Praise for the Pray for Me Campaign and Prayer Guide

The focus on prayer really sets the campaign apart and gives any adult believer the opportunity to make a difference in the life of a teenager. What better starting place for a true, deep connection between generations that will make a lasting difference in the lives of young people? My prayer is that churches everywhere would seriously consider making the Pray for Me Campaign a strategic part of how they minister to the next generation.
Doug Fields, Author, Speaker, Youth Pastor, Co-Founder, Downloadyouthministry.com

The Pray for Me Campaign is a grassroots movement that brings students and adults together spiritually. Far too many young people are leaving the church in their teen years and this campaign has the makings of a renewal that will help this generation of young people stay grounded in their faith. Tony Souder is a wonderful Christian leader who is exactly the right person to lead this movement. I hope this campaign grabs hold of our hearts and becomes one of the next great renewals in the church worldwide.
Dr. Jim Burns, President, HomeWord, Author of Confident Parenting

This is a simple, clearly organized, biblically focused, and powerful way to involve adults in students' lives. I highly commend it to you.
Dr. Dann Spader, President, Global Youth Initiative, Founder, Sonlife Ministries, Author of 4 Chair Discipling

The Pray for Me Campaign is a brilliant and much-needed bridge over the frighteningly wide gap between adults that care and this generation of students. My friend Tony Souder, an elite youth ministry veteran and proven leader, keenly understands that the role of an adult is indispensible in passing on a sustainable faith to a teenager. As the parent of three teenagers, I cannot recommend this resource more highly.

Stuart Hall, Orange Leader, Communicator, Coauthor of The Seven Checkpoints and Max Q

The research is clear. For teenagers to carry the aroma of Jesus at age 18 and to walk in faith for a lifetime, they each need to be connected to at least five godly adults. In every book I write and every talk I give, I present the fact that one of those needs to be a Prayer Champion. Tony Souder and his team have created tools and channels for calling and equipping adults for just that role. The Pray for Me Campaign and those behind it are trustworthy partners in youth ministry. They have my full endorsement.

Dr. Richard Ross, Professor of Student Ministry at Southwestern Seminary

Tony Souder has offered the people of God a Christ-centered and God-attentive approach to youth ministry that simply thrills my heart and convicts my soul. I can't remember the last time that I saw prayer as the point of the arrow for ministry to students. I suppose the last place I have seen it was in the Word of God itself. I thank [Tony] for the model and the manner in which he has written. I commend this to you without reservation and with great excitement.

Joseph V. Novenson, Senior Teaching Pastor, Lookout Mountain Presbyterian Church

Having experienced forty years of student ministry, I have seen many great ideas and utilized many great materials to engage teens for Christ's glory. Occasionally there is a resource that combines a unique idea with exceptional materials that is able to impact students and usher student ministry to a whole new level. The Pray for Me Campaign along with the accompanying Prayer Guide do just that.

Matt Brinkley, Founder and CEO of PACT Ministry

Many churches and ministries have begun to awaken to the power and richness of intergenerational ministry, and yet implementation has been quite the challenge for the local church. The Pray for Me Campaign is one of the most exciting and practical ways of connecting the generations that I can think of. The greatest beauty is that this movement leans on the power of the Holy Spirit and not a program.

Nate Stratman, Coauthor of Building Your Volunteer Team, Sticky Faith Coach, Ministry Architects Consultant

Pray for Me

THE PRAYER CHAMPION'S
GUIDE TO ESSENTIAL PRAYER FOR
THE NEXT GENERATION

Tony Souder

Read Avenue Press

CHATTANOOGA, TN

Tony Souder/Read Avenue Press
P.O. Box 2468
Chattanooga, Tennessee/37409
PrayforMeCampaign.com

Book Layout ©2013 BookDesignTemplates.com

Cover Design by Nathan Mileur and Allison Dowlen

Pray for Me: The Prayer Champion's Guide to Essential Prayer for the Next Generation/ Tony Souder. —1st ed.
ISBN 978-0-9897545-4-5

Contents

This book is dedicated to my wife, Rhonda.
No one has loved me more or prayed for me better!

ACKNOWLEDGEMENTS

First, I want to thank my three biggest fans: my wife, Rhonda, and my twin daughters, Abby and Bethany. Your encouragement, love, and laughter are just three of Jesus' good gifts that help me stay the course. Thank you!

Because this book is all about making a difference in the next generation during their formative years, I want to give a special nod to three outstanding couples who were instrumental in my seeing, savoring, and sharing Jesus in my formative years as a believer. Owen and Barbara Lupton played a decisive role in introducing me to my Savior, as well as investing countless hours discipling me in the early years. Bob and Jean Ackiss took me in and loved me as their own all through college and beyond. Their home was a haven. My soul was stabilized by the sweetness of Jesus that these two soaked me in as a young man. I also want to recognize Lewis and DeLena Baker, who are now both basking in the wonder of heaven with the lover of their souls. Their commitment to Jesus, young people, and the church in rural North Carolina for over five decades has produced a host of God-honoring lovers of Jesus. Their prayer-saturated lives will forever mark me.

I also want to take time to thank those who have helped make this book a reality. Thank you to all the gracious friends who read, reflected, and helped make revisions that have resulted in a much better resource for the Church. Thank you to Corrie Walker, a Communications major from Bryan College who provided significant editorial excellence for the project. Special thanks go to Megan DeMoss, who I believe was raised up for such a time as this. Your contribution to the overall project has been a clear provision from God. You have been a rock star for the cause.

Lastly, I want to thank all those who have made it possible for the Chattanooga Youth Network to serve our region's youth ministry effort since 1994. You know who you are; you are our financial partners, board, and staff members, both past and present. Thanks for making twenty years of effective ministry possible. Thanks also to the thousands of youth leaders, both paid and volunteer, who have faithfully served the teenagers in our region. May your tribe increase!

The Pray for Me Campaign is ultimately about the Church passing on the wonder and majesty of Jesus Christ to each emerging generation in a natural and sustainable way. Unfortunately, we know from national research that we as the church in the United States are struggling in our effectiveness to do so. The scope of teens drifting from the church is seen in the following research from Sticky Faith:

- 40-50% of students *from good youth groups and families* will drift from God and the church after high school (Drs. Kara E. Powell and Chap Clark [Zondervan: 2011])

Some researchers say as many as 80% will walk away by age 29. There are complex reasons behind the large number of young people drifting from the church, but there is a very clear factor uniting all of those who remain connected to the church and flourish in their faith: they have one or more adult believers intentionally investing in their lives. Dr. Powell highlights Dr. Clark's brilliance on this factor in *Sticky Faith*:

Many children's and youth ministries say they want to have a 1:5 ratio of adults to kids (meaning they want one adult for every five kids) for their Sunday school class or small groups. What if we reversed that? What if we said we want a 5:1 adult-to-kid ratio—five caring adults for each kid?... We're talking about five adults whom you recruit to invest in your kid in little, medium, and big ways. (p. 101)

The National Study of Youth and Religion, along with the entire scope of Scripture, also points to the indispensible role of adult believers in commending the greatness of God to the next generation.

Psalm 145:4 says, "One generation shall commend your works to another and shall declare your mighty acts." Psalm 71:17-18 says, "O God, from my youth you have taught me, and I still proclaim your wondrous deeds. So even to old age and gray hairs, O God, do not forsake me, until I proclaim your might to another generation, your power to all those to come." Both of these passages make it clear that adults, as a collective and as individuals, are compelled to declare the greatness of God to the next generation. But in spite of what we know to be true in Scripture and extensive national studies, we still have an incredibly difficult time motivating and empowering adult believers to effectively commend Jesus to the next generation.

This is where the Pray for Me Campaign comes in. The Pray for Me Campaign is designed to get more adults engaging naturally with more teenagers about things that matter. The plan is simply to help every teenager who is touched by the Church to invite three adult believers from three different generations to become their Prayer Champions for the school year. These Prayer Champions will pray using this book, which empowers them to pray effectively for their student during the entire school year.

Why three adults from three different generations? It is rare for a person to flourish in any part of their life with just one person on their team. Our desire is that every teenager would have a team of Prayer Champions that represents the scope of the Body of Christ. We believe that passing on a genuine faith is most effective when we can taste the sweetness of following Jesus from every generation.

The Pray for Me Campaign is a strategic step in mobilizing adults from every generation to intentionally begin investing in the lives of teenagers in a natural way. We have taken the most basic of Christian acts—prayer—and made it the connecting point between generations. We have seen countless times how prayer provides an easy and non-threatening way to initiate relationships across generational lines, and yet also creates a bond that is supernatural and lasting. May God be pleased in establishing relationships across generational lines throughout his entire Church. May our effectiveness in offering a clear picture of the beauty and majesty of Jesus to the next generation increase a hundredfold. Thank you for your role in this grand endeavor!

PRAY FOR ME CAMPAIGN OVERVIEW:
a simple way of investing in the next generation through prayer

ONE
STUDENT
INVITES

FROM
THREE
GENERATIONS

WHO ALL COMMIT TO
PRAYING
THROUGH THE GUIDE

THREE
ADULT BELIEVERS

TO BE HIS OR HER
PRAYER
CHAMPIONS

FOR ONE
ENTIRE SCHOOL YEAR

THE VISION: THAT EVERY YOUNG PERSON IN THE CHURCH WOULD HAVE A TEAM OF ADULT BELIEVERS SERVING AS THEIR PRAYER CHAMPIONS.

You may have this Prayer Guide in your hands because your church is launching the Pray for Me Campaign. Or, you may have come across this book on your own, and you are using it for your own personal prayer life. Regardless, the Prayer Guide is created to help empower individuals, and entire churches to invest in the next generation through prayer. If your church hasn't launched the campaign, perhaps you are the person to bring Pray for Me to them and help strengthen the intergenerational relationships within your church. Interested in learning more?

Visit our website: prayformecampaign.com

Before God enables his people to bring in a harvest, he pours out a Spirit of prayer upon them. The surest sign that God is about to send power upon us is a great movement of prayer in our midst.

—JOHN PIPER

The Invitation

I was 17 when I accepted Christ as my Savior. I remember walking into church during those first few weeks after becoming a Christian. Adults repeatedly expressed their happiness for me, saying that they had been praying for me. As a newbie follower of Christ coming from a non-Christian home, I was clueless concerning the scope of what they were saying. When I reflect on what their prayers meant to me in those early days, several clear memories come to mind. First, I was shocked that I was on the radar of any of these people. After all, I was really a stranger to them. I was doubly surprised that they would take the time to pray for me. I also remember that surprise being swallowed up by a very strong sense of love and care from these adults. Their willingness to pray for me, and their expressions of care and concern, transformed the trajectory of my life. Though I was young, I did realize I had walked into a massive amount of goodness, and I liked it—a lot! The "goodness" that I had walked into was the Body of Christ, filled with people who knew God and wanted me to know him. God loves to use the private and public prayers of his people to change the world, to change a teenager's world, like mine.

You have been invited. You have been offered an incredible gift. A teenager has opened the door to their life by offering you a simple invitation to pray for them. By inviting you to pray for them, they have built an invisible bridge of relationship between you and them. Your acceptance of their offer allows you the freedom to cross that bridge to naturally engage with them along the way. This book exists to help you fulfill your commitment to be their Prayer Champion. You may not yet feel like a Prayer Champion, but your acceptance of their invitation is a great affirmation that you are. This book will guide you in pleading for God's provision, protection, presence, and purposes to be established in their lives. When we begin to pray like this for others, something amazing happens inside of us as well. Our hearts become larger toward God and others. We begin to move toward others to bless and encourage them in ways beyond prayer. This book is designed with that in mind. Our hope is that you will find uncontainable joy in praying Scripture over the next generation. We also hope that you will respond with a resounding "Yes!" if and when God leads you to invest in their lives in other ways as well. We believe a wave of God's goodness will follow the prayers of his people. Let the goodness begin.

"Will you pray for me?" is such a simple request and yet it is too often not taken seriously enough. I would like to say that I have felt the full weight of each request when someone has asked me to pray for them, but that simply is not true. Regrettably, there have been times when I have not given the plea for prayer a second thought. Fortunately, my attentiveness to prayer was transformed one day when I was sitting in a hospital room after my wife's surgery in Long Island, New York. It wasn't like I was looking for transformation that day; I was minding my own business, reading through the Gospel of Matthew, when God opened my eyes to see a truth that in my blindness I had overlooked every other time I had read the familiar passage found in chapter 7:7-12.

Ask and it will be given to you; seek, and you will find; knock, and it will be opened to you. For everyone who asks receives, and the one who seeks finds, and to the one who knocks it will be opened. Or which one of you, if his son asks him for bread, will give him a stone? Or if he asks for a fish, will give him a serpent? If you then, who are evil, know how to give good gifts to your children, how much more will your Father who is in heaven give good things to those who ask him! (Matthew 7:7-11)

I am very confident that you know the next verse, and yet, you may be surprised to find it here, in this context. It is The Golden Rule: "So whatever you wish that others would do to you, do also to them, for this is the Law and the Prophets" (Matthew 7:12).

Jesus put The Golden Rule right at the culminating point of a passage about deliberate, persistent, hopeful prayer. So here is my takeaway from that hospital room years ago: Jesus wants us to approach prayer for others with the same intensity and hopeful expectation as we would want them to approach praying for us. The Golden Rule can be used as a means to bring intensity and hopeful expectation to your prayers for others, especially your children, grandchildren, and the youth within our churches.

The Pray for Me Campaign is about hope, specifically the hope that teenagers can find in the greatness of God. Every generation needs to find their greatest hope, satisfaction, and enjoyment in God. This Campaign will help you lead teenagers to this hope through prayer. It is through prayer that the Holy Spirit sustains and strengthens our personal walk with God. It is designed to help adult believers call out to God for his loving provision, protection, presence, and purpose in the lives of the next generation. The Campaign has three aims:

1. Help the next generation see and savor the greatness of God through the prayers of God's people.
2. Help adult believers see themselves as Prayer Champions who intentionally pray for and invest in the next generation.
3. Create a web of multi-generational relationships in which one generation would share the greatness of God with another.

Strategic Prayer

There are plenty of books out there about praying for others. What makes this one different? For starters, the prayers in this book are specifically geared towards the next generation. More importantly, this guide is designed to give your prayers focus, clarity, and consistency. There are three primary components whose combined uniqueness provide traction for this prayer guide:

- Praying the Scriptures
- The 7 Essentials
- SeeSavorShare (S3)

Praying the Scriptures

This prayer guide is rooted and established in the truths of Scripture. The Bible is the Word of God and as such has the power to give life to us and our prayers. Throughout this book you will learn how to turn Scripture into prayers for the next generation. Praying Scripture is one of the most powerful and authoritative ways to pray. Let's take a moment to be reminded of some of the promises that await us as we soak in the Scriptures.

The Word of God:
- Gives life (Psalm 119:25, 107)
- Strengthens (Psalm 119:28)
- Guards from sin and keeps us pure (Psalm 119:9, 11)
- Creates and sustains the universe (Psalm 33:6, 2 Peter 3:5, Hebrews 1:3, 11:3)
- Creates spiritual life (1 Peter 1:23, James 1:18)
- Is able to save our souls (James 1:21)
- Is living and active and able to discern the thoughts and intentions of the heart (Hebrews 4:12)
- Produces faith (Romans 10:17)
- Teaches, reproves, corrects, and trains in righteousness (2 Timothy 3:16)

These passages offer a taste of the goodness that flows from the supremacy and power of the Word of God.

One of the compelling aspects about the Pray for Me Prayer Guide is that it takes the most powerful words in the world, the very words of God, and makes them the catalyst for our prayers for the next generation. The apostle Paul refers to the Scriptures as the Sword of the Spirit, and we know from Hebrews 4:12 that "the word of God is living and active, sharper than any two-edged sword, piercing to the division of soul and of spirit, of joints and of marrow, and discerning the thoughts and intentions of the heart." God uses his Word to transform our hearts whether it is written, spoken, or uttered silently in prayer to the Father. In this prayer guide I am committed to letting the very truths of Scripture be the fodder for our prayers. We will take passages of Scripture that relate to each of The 7 Essentials and turn them into life-giving prayers for the next generation.

Praying like the Psalmist Prays

It would be hard to have a Scripture-centered prayer guide that didn't in some way point to the primary prayer and songbook in the Bible. Therefore, we will be taking cues from the Psalms in our efforts to turn Scriptures into prayers. They reveal a plethora of ways to plead with God. There is a grittiness and authenticity in the Psalms that promotes clarity, honesty, urgency, and directness. Let's look at a few phrases from Psalm 119 that can give us a glimpse into the psalmist's directness and dependence on God in prayer:

- Do good to your servant (17)
- Open my eyes that I may see (18)
- Remove from me scorn... (22)
- Preserve my life according to your word (25)
- Teach me your decrees (26)
- Let me understand the teaching of your precepts (27)
- Strengthen me (28)
- Keep me from deceitful ways (29)
- Do not let me be put to shame (31)
- Give me... (34)
- Direct me... (35)
- Turn my heart... (36)
- Turn my eyes... (37)
- Fulfill your promise... (38)
- Take away... (39)
- May your unfailing love... (41)
- Do not snatch your word from my mouth (43)
- Remember... (49)
- Be gracious (58)

- Let your compassion… (77)

Each of these phrases is a clear call for God to act; a plea for the favor of God to act on the psalmists' behalf. As we turn Scripture into prayer for the next generation, we are ushering a clear call for God to act on their behalf. May God be ever so gracious to act and intervene for the good of the next generation! May he cause us to be relentless in our prayers and our intentionality in bringing his greatness to the next generation. May God soften their hearts to his greatness and grant them faithful responsiveness to his Word and to us as Prayer Champions as we care for them.

The 7 Essentials

This prayer guide is structured around what I call The 7 Essentials. These seven aspects of life are the minimum essentials that I believe need to be attended to for someone to flourish in living faithfully before God and man.

The 7 Essentials come directly from two passages of the Bible, but their importance saturates all of Scripture. The first two, wisdom and favor, come from Luke 2:52: "And Jesus increased in wisdom and in stature and in favor with God and man." It is not surprising that Jesus grew in wisdom and favor because he was God in human form. What is surprising is that Luke makes sure that we know Jesus grew in wisdom and favor. Luke could have said anything he wanted about Jesus, but he made a point to let us know that wisdom and favor with God and man were essential, even for the Son of God. If it was essential for God's Son to grow in wisdom and favor, then there is no question that these two are essential for us. The other five Essentials are found in 1

Timothy 4:12: "Let no one despise you for your youth, but set the believers an example in speech, in conduct, in love, in faith, in purity." It is crucial to understand that Paul is not using throwaway words here. He is giving Timothy the essential categories that he needs to pay attention to in order to set an appropriate example for all believers. There was a lot at stake in this simple and precise directive from Paul to Timothy. These categories remain essential for us today.

In this prayer guide The 7 Essentials have been arranged into three categories based on the role of each Essential:

- The Favor Foundation: Favor
- The Core Four: Wisdom, Love, Faith, and Purity
- The Public Relations (PR) Pair: Speech and Conduct

The Favor Foundation

As I write this, a 408-foot spire is being lifted to the top of the new One World Trade Center in New York City making it the tallest building in the Western Hemisphere at 1,776 feet. Its stunning structure graces the Manhattan skyline. As we marvel at the grandeur of such a structure, how often do we take time to consider its foundation? Foundations are easily forgotten and yet they are indispensable. Often times we forget that God's favor is the foundation of our lives. It is a strong and secure foundation, but in this world that values self-reliance, it is easy to forget that we are completely dependent on him. Think of God's favor as anything he does in, through, or for you. We can see the favor of God in his provision, protection, presence, and purposes.

He [Jesus] is the image of the invisible God, the firstborn of creation. For by Jesus all things were created, in heaven and on earth, visible and invisible, whether thrones or dominions or rulers or authorities— all things were created through Jesus and for Jesus. And Jesus is before all things, and in Jesus all things hold together. (Colossians 1:15-17)

Our entire existence results from God's creating and sustaining favor. This is the foundation for all the other Essentials. What does a teenager need to recognize God's favor in their lives? They need eyes to see, ears to hear, and humble hearts to understand and embrace the favor of God for all it is worth. We must be diligent in praying that the next generation develops a posture of humility so that they might see the favor of God in his provision, protection, presence, and purposes.

The Core Four

I call wisdom, love, faith, and purity the Core Four because they reflect the condition of our hearts. They represent the substance of who we are. It is in these areas that we need God to unleash his favor first and foremost. We need:

1. *Wisdom.* The young people we are praying for are making decisions every day that will affect the rest of their lives. It is our desire that God would use our prayers to enhance their wisdom in order to make good decisions—and to reduce their regrets when they don't. We should look to the book of Proverbs and the person of Jesus as we pray for wisdom to take root in the next generation. Proverbs specifically seeks to provide "knowledge and discretion to the youth" (Proverbs 1:4).

In Colossians 2:3, Paul says that "in [Jesus] are hidden all the treasures of wisdom and knowledge." As we pray for these teenagers' relationship with Jesus to deepen, we are also addressing their need for greater and greater wisdom.

2. *Love.* God is love. Love for God and others is the crux on which all the law and prophets hang according to Matthew 22:37-40:

And he said to him, "You shall love the Lord your God with all your heart and with all your soul and with all your mind. This is the great and first commandment. And a second is like it: You shall love your neighbor as yourself. On these two commandments depend all the Law and the Prophets."

Love is what transforms us. That is why the apostle Paul was so intentional in Ephesians 3:18-19, praying that believers "may have strength to comprehend with all the saints what is the breadth and length and height and depth, and to know the love of Christ that surpasses knowledge, that you may be filled with all the fullness of God."

3. *Faith.* Faith is the gift of God's favor that makes salvation possible (Ephesians 2:8-9). Faith is absolutely necessary in pleasing God. Hebrews 11:6 says, "[W]ithout faith it is impossible to please him, for whoever would draw near to God must believe that he exists and that he rewards those who seek him."

4. *Purity.* Blessing and favor of God follow the pure in heart. God gives us vision to see him as we pursue a life of purity. Matthew 5:8 says, "Blessed are the pure in

heart, for they shall see God." As we pray for the next generation it is essential that we seek God's favor to cause their wisdom, love, faith, and purity to flourish.

The PR Pair: Speech and Conduct

I love watching the award-winning specials produced by National Geographic. The clarity of nature that they are able to capture is stunning. I am specifically reminded of a photograph of an iceberg in Pleneau Bay off Pleneau Island, which is close to the Antarctic Circle. The photograph was a split shot view capturing a unique image of the iceberg both above and below the waterline. It brought the phrase "tip of the iceberg" to life. Scientists state that because of the density of ice, only ten percent of an iceberg is visible above water, while the bulk of its substance sits below the surface. When you think about it, we are actually a lot like icebergs. People around us get to see about ten percent of who we really are through our speech and conduct—yet there is so much more to us that is "under the waterline." In some ways, our speech and conduct are like high-tech animated billboards above the surface sending messages to all who pass by saying, "This is who we are!" and "This is what we are made of!" Like all messages from billboards, our speech and conduct only serve as signs of who we are below the surface. They give clues, but they don't share the whole story. They are just the tip of the iceberg.

It is in our speech and conduct that we "go public" with who we are, or at least who we want people to *think* we are, on the inside. Our wisdom, love, faith, and purity are forged on the inside and then expressed on the outside in what we say and do. This is where the rubber meets the road in our Christian lives. The importance of our speech and conduct cannot be overstated.

The goal is for what we say and do to accurately reflect who we are on the inside. It is through what we say and do that we offer the world a clear or hazy picture of God. We were created by God to magnify his greatness by our lips and by our lives.

I want to challenge you with two simple questions to help guide you in becoming an authentic follower of Christ in both your speech and conduct. These questions are designed to shine a light on the state of your hearts and to direct you toward an ever-increasing dependence on God.

1. *Am I playing the part without the heart?* God's greatest desire for us is that we would love him with all our heart, soul, mind, and strength, and that we would love others as ourselves. This question points to our propensity to pretend that he is our treasure when other things are our pleasure. Jesus saved some of his most scathing words for those who honored him with their lips while their hearts were far from him. Let this question do its good work and prompt us toward having a heart that is captured by God and his greatness.

2. *Am I allowing my speech and conduct to fulfill their purpose in my spiritual growth?* Our speech and conduct have several purposes—to communicate to the world who we are and what we stand for, and to communicate with ourselves. Are you listening to what your speech and conduct are telling you about the spiritual condition of your heart? As Christians, we have the Holy Spirit living in us and letting us know when we say or do something that is out of sync with either who we are or who God calls us to be. It is crucial that we listen to the Spirit's convictions and promptings. We must be

careful not to resist and quench the Holy Spirit's working within us. We must listen to the Holy Spirit when he brings our sin and inconsistencies to light and respond by confessing and forsaking them by his power. This is one of the key ways in which we are conformed to the image of Jesus, which is God's ultimate purpose for our lives.

The SeeSavorShare Discipleship Process

As you launch into this prayer guide, I want to introduce you to a simple process that can help your walk with God flourish. It is the SeeSavorShare (S3) discipleship process, which is the third component that makes this prayer guide unique. Over the last decade S3 has become the rhythm of my life with God, and I would like to encourage you to embrace it as your own as well. First, I want to give a little background concerning the value and necessity of S3. I have been a follower of Christ since 1978, but in March of 1995 God enrolled my wife and me in an intensive spiritual growth course. It was at that time that my wife began having severe migraine-like headaches. Over the next eighteen years, with three major surgeries and fifty-plus doctors from all across the country in our rearview mirror, her pain has not decreased but expanded to include intense muscle and bone pain that has caused countless tear-filled nights.

We have experienced the full spectrum of Western, Eastern, conventional, and unconventional medical approaches. From a Christian spiritual perspective we have experienced the full spectrum of biblical prayer and healing efforts on both individual and corporate levels. It has been in this extended season of suffering that I have had to learn to walk with God in a new way. Anyone can live for God when the wind is at his or her back and all is well, but this was not my experience. I was constantly being called on to be more than I had capacity to fulfill, and the S3 discipleship process became, and still is, my spiritual survival process. Thankfully, you do not have to experience eighteen-plus years of suffering to begin seeing, savoring, and sharing the greatness of God that is all around you. You can begin the process today. S3 is the intentional process of looking for God in all of life. It is a thrilling way to walk with God and fuel a lavish love for him and others, regardless of your circumstances. It is God's desire for us to see his goodness, kindness, mercy, faithfulness, and love in all of life's situations. As he gives us a vision of his greatness in our lives, we must savor it for all it is worth with thanksgiving, praise, and adoration. It is out of the overflow of our savoring that we share freely with others daily. This process can send life deep into your soul, just as taking in oxygen brings life to the body. S3 can become the rhythm of your life with God.

At the very core of S3 are three powerful truths:

1. Everything God does is great, so everything we see about who God is, what he is doing, or has done should be savored and shared.
2. We can see the greatness of God in Scripture, our daily lives, and in all of creation.
3. The Bible is the only reliable source for understanding what is true about God and what he is doing in our lives and the world around us.

Seeing

Seeing the greatness of God is the first step. The greatness of his character and works can be seen all around us. It is God's desire that we see all of the various aspects of his greatness. He wants our hearts and minds to be captured by the magnificence of his holiness, justice, righteousness, power, wisdom, goodness, patience, kindness, faithfulness, gentleness, and love. His wonders are endless! If our relationship with God ever grows stale, it is not because he is not grand enough to capture the expanse of our hearts; it is because we are blind to the fullness of his beauty. Just as blind Bartimaeus diligently pursued Jesus to give him sight (Mark 10:46-52), so must we be intentional in asking God to give us spiritual sight to see his greatness all around us. Here are some things to remember about seeing God's greatness:

- We can see his greatness in Scripture, life, and creation.
- We can see, hear, and understand what he empowers us to, so one of our constant prayers must be for God to give us eyes to see, ears to hear, and hearts to understand his will and working in this world.

Savoring

Savoring the greatness of God that we see in Scripture, life, and creation is the next step of S3. Savoring is the heart's response to what we are seeing of God. Savoring is essential to our growth with God because it is about enjoying and delighting in God and his greatness. Savoring moves us away from simply having intellectual knowledge of God; it moves us closer to personally knowing him and what he cares about. It moves us closer because sustained savoring expands our heart's capacity to love God. Here are some things to remember about savoring God's greatness:

- Savoring is essential because we pursue what we love with purpose and intensity.
- Savoring takes time. We have to slow down and ponder what we have seen.
- Giving thanks, delighting, and treasuring are key aspects of savoring.
- Begin savoring by recalling times or places in your life where you have seen God's presence, protection, or provision.

Sharing

Sharing about God is the natural overflow of seeing and savoring his greatness. Sharing actually plays two primary roles for us in our growth with God. First, it completes the enjoyment of what we have seen and savored. When we see something incredible, we immediately begin looking for someone to share it with. Sharing is the culminating point in enjoying the greatness of God we have seen. Second, sharing helps us see what has a hold on our hearts. We naturally talk about what we love and enjoy. S3 is designed to help us deepen our love and enjoyment in God by seeing, savoring, and ultimately sharing his greatness with others. Here are a few things to remember about sharing God's greatness:

- Pay attention to what you talk about most. This can give you some insight into what holds the most space in your heart. The goal in this process is that you would begin to see and savor the greatness of God in your life, and sharing would naturally become the next step.

- To begin sharing, engage others about where they have seen God at work in their lives. Most people will have a time or place where they would say God has worked in their life.

- Be prepared to share stories about how you've seen God's greatness in your life. Sharing deepens your relationship with God in Christ. Philemon 6 says, "I pray that the sharing of your faith may become effective for the full knowledge of every good thing that is in us for the sake of Christ." This is a great encouragement and promise! This means every time we ask someone to share how God has worked in their lives, we are providing a means of establishing them in their faith. So don't hesitate to share, and don't hesitate to ask others to share!

S3 is included in this prayer guide to bring the abstract truth about God into the present reality of your life. When we pray for the next generation, we must remember to pray with a vision of their being captured by the greatness of God. Each day we will pray one of The 7 Essentials using S3 as our lens to help provide focus and clarity for these prayers. May God grant us favor to see and savor his greatness in Scripture, life, and creation, so we will be ready to convey it to the next generation. Let's pray that God would unleash his favor in and through the next generation!

Make the Prayers Your Own!

As you begin your journey through the prayers in this guide, remember to make them your own! Each prayer is written in plural form to allow you ease in praying for several people at once. There will be a tendency to read through the prayers in a rote manner; resist this tendency. Hover over the words and phrases and soak in their meaning. Find freedom in expanding and enhancing the prayers as you offer them to God.

The 7 Essentials in 7 Days

Every day is designed to provide you with a clear and fresh opportunity for engaging God in Scripture through prayer for your student. You'll notice, however, that each prayer is written in the plural tense so you can pray for more than one individual. It is our hope that you will pray for your student as well as anyone God may put on your heart.

The S3 life and ministry model guides you through each day, prompting you with ways to see, savor, and share the fullness of God. The *see* portion is a passage of Scripture where you can circle or underline words and phrases that stand out to you. Next, you will *savor* those truths in prayer for your student. Finally, you will have the opportunity to record any thoughts or ideas that were pressed into your heart during the see and savor portions. It is our hope and expectation that you will *share* them with someone else!

Before you launch into the daily prayers portion, flip to the Appendix on page 146 and check out the "Ten Tips for Engaging with Teens." This section is filled with practical ways to begin forming a relationship with your student naturally and effectively.

Day One: Favor

Father, open my eyes so that I might *see* you more clearly, *savor* you more fully, and *share* you more freely.

Circle or underline any key words or phrases you *See*:

Yours, O LORD, is the greatness and the power and the glory and the victory and the majesty, for all that is in the heavens and in the earth is yours. Yours is the kingdom, O LORD, and you are exalted as head above all. Both riches and honor come from you, and you rule over all. In your hand are power and might, and in your hand it is to make great and to give strength to all. And now we thank you, our God, and praise your glorious name. (1 Chronicles 29:11-13)

Savor these truths in prayer for you and your student:

Father, you are great and worthy to be praised. I pray that _____ would know and embrace your favor and never stop growing in wonder and amazement of your greatness. Awaken their hearts and minds to comprehend that all goodness flows from your hand. When they look at the heavens, cause them to know the heavens are yours! When they look in the mirror, cause them to know that they are yours. Create in them a relentless reliance on you and your provisions of favor in all of life. Enable them to be enthralled by you as the giver of all things. Give them exuberant praise and thankfulness at the thought of your glorious name. For your glory and their good, in the sovereign name of Jesus, amen.

Write down any thoughts or ideas you may want to *Share*:

Day Two: Wisdom

Father, open my eyes so that I might *see* you more clearly, *savor* you more fully, and *share* you more freely.

Circle or underline any key words or phrases you *See*:

So teach us to number our days that we may get a heart of wisdom. (Psalm 90:12)

O Lord, make me know my end and what is the measure of my days; let me know how fleeting I am! (Psalm 39:4)

Savor these truths in prayer for you and your student:

Father, it is so easy for days and years to pass by before we realize they are gone. I pray for _____, that you would help them realize how precious each moment is. Teach them to savor every day as a gift from you and help them to live each day with purposeful intentionality. Cause them to understand that their lives are sustained by you. Help them to realize this life is also fleeting, so they should always seek to follow you faithfully. Give them a long-term view of life so they can make wise short-term decisions. Remind them that it is in living for you that their lives become the most fulfilling. For your glory and their good, in Jesus' name, amen.

Write down any thoughts or ideas you may want to *Share*:

Day Three: Love

Father, open my eyes so that I might *see* you more clearly, *savor* you more fully, and *share* you more freely.

Circle or underline any key words or phrases you *See*:

For God so loved the world, that he gave his only Son, that whoever believes in him should not perish but have eternal life. (John 3:16)

For while we were still weak, at the right time Christ died for the ungodly. For one will scarcely die for a righteous person—though perhaps for a good person one would dare even to die—but God shows his love for us in that while we were still sinners, Christ died for us. (Romans 5:6-8)

Savor these truths in prayer for you and your student:

Father, thank you for loving us so much that you gave up your only Son. Your love is overwhelmingly sacrificial! Words are inadequate to express the magnitude of your love. It staggers the mind to think that you loved us when we had nothing to offer. There was nothing attractive about us. We were sinners, rebelling against all of your goodness and majesty. Cause _____ to be captured by the depth and sweetness of your sacrificial love. Let it soak deep into their hearts. Cause it to empower them to live sacrificial, loving lives. For your glory and their good, in Jesus' name, amen.

Write down any thoughts or ideas you may want to *Share*:

Day Four: Faith

Father, open my eyes so that I might *see* you more clearly, *savor* you more fully, and *share* you more freely.

Circle or underline any key words or phrases you *See*:

Trust in the LORD with all your heart, and do not lean on your own understanding. In all your ways acknowledge him, and he will make straight your paths. (Proverbs 3:5-6)

Savor these truths in prayer for you and your student:

Father, life is so often complex and confusing. I thank you for your promises that provide hope and clarity in the midst of life's complexity. Today I pray that _____ would place their trust in you, surrendering every aspect of their lives to you, believing that you love them. Empower them to fight the urge to trust in their own understanding more than they rely on you and your guidance. Cause them to look to you in all their ways, acknowledging their need for, dependence on, and hope in you. Help them to acknowledge all of your provisions as they see you make their paths straight. Give them eyes to see the wonders you perform as they surrender and yield to your purposes. You are their God! Help them treasure you today with every breath, and cause them to call others to treasure you with all of their hearts as well. For your glory and their good, in Jesus' name, amen!

Write down any thoughts or ideas you may want to *Share*:

Day Five: Purity

Father, open my eyes so that I might *see* you more clearly, *savor* you more fully, and *share* you more freely.

Circle or underline any key words or phrases you *See*:

How can a young man keep his way pure? By guarding it according to your word. With my whole heart I seek you; let me not wander from your commandments! I have stored up your word in my heart, that I might not sin against you. (Psalm 119:9-11)

Savor these truths in prayer for you and your student:

Father, in a world that disregards purity, the question of the psalmist is vital: "How can a young man [or woman] keep their way pure?" A wholehearted pursuit of you and your Word is the answer. I pray that _____ would taste the sweetness of Scripture and desire it with their whole hearts. Help them to believe that your Word is the Sword of the Spirit that can lead, guide, and empower them to pursue purity in every decision. Give them the desire and will to hide your Word in their hearts that they might not sin against you. Holy, holy, holy is the Lord God Almighty. In Jesus' name, amen.

Write down any thoughts or ideas you may want to *Share*:

Day Six: Speech

Father, open my eyes so that I might *see* you more clearly, *savor* you more fully, and *share* you more freely.

Circle or underline any key words or phrases you *See*:

It is good to give to thanks to the LORD, to sing praises to your name, O Most High; to declare your steadfast love in the morning, and your faithfulness by night... (Psalm 92:1-2)

Savor these truths in prayer for you and your student:

Father, I praise you today. You are great and glorious. Help _____ to use their words to give you thanks for all you are and all you do. Let their hearts sing songs of praise to your name. Give them understanding of your great love for them each morning. May their words declare your steadfast love. Help them to see and savor the truth that every day they are walking into the care and love of their heavenly father. Grant them the ability to recognize your faithfulness throughout each day, using their speech to give thanks and praise your great name. For your glory and their good, in Jesus' name, amen.

Write down any thoughts or ideas you may want to *Share*:

Day Seven: Conduct

Father, open my eyes so that I might *see* you more clearly, *savor* you more fully, and *share* you more freely.

Circle or underline any key words or phrases you *See*:

He has told you, O man, what is good; and what does the LORD require of you but to do justice, and to love kindness, and to walk humbly with your God? (Micah 6:8)

Savor these truths in prayer for you and your student:

Father, you have told us what is good and what you require of us. You have made it plain that you desire for us to do justice, love kindness, and walk humbly with you all of our days. I pray that _____ would take these three commands to heart and pursue them with reckless abandon. Make them alert to attend to the weak and less fortunate. Do not let them turn a blind eye to injustice when it is in their power to act. Awaken their hearts and minds to the needs for love and mercy all around them. Create in them the ability to meet those needs. As they seek to promote justice and to love kindness in this world, empower them to do it humbly before you and man. For your glory and their good, in Jesus' name, amen.

Write down any thoughts or ideas you may want to *Share*:

Notes

The 7 Essentials in 7 Days

By now you are getting into the rhythm of praying for your young friend. You have just prayed a week of the 7 Essentials over them. Only God knows the extent of goodness he is bringing their way because of your prayers. As you begin praying a second week for your student, remember to pay attention to what God brings to the forefront of your mind. I tend to see these prayers as "spark" prayers. God can use these prayers as a spark of his goodness to ignite a blaze of ongoing prayer for your friend and others throughout the day. Let any thoughts or ideas you may have prompt you to drill down deeper in prayer. It could be that at the end of each prayer you ask yourself:

What one thing would I add to this prayer for my friend?
Or:
What is today's takeaway thought for ongoing prayer?

Day One: Favor

Father, open my eyes so that I might *see* you more clearly, *savor* you more fully, and *share* you more freely.

Circle or underline any key words or phrases you *See*:

For by grace you have been saved through faith. And this is not your own doing; it is the gift of God, not a result of works, so that no one may boast. For we are his workmanship, created in Christ Jesus for good works, which God prepared beforehand, that we should walk in them. (Ephesians 2:8-10)

Savor these truths in prayer for you and your student:

Father, thank you that salvation is a gift. Thank you that it is not based on our good works, but on Jesus' perfect work on the cross. I pray that you would give _____ greater faith to trust you for their salvation. Protect them from the deception of thinking and acting as if they can earn or add to their salvation by doing good works. Cause them to know that they are your workmanship, created in Jesus Christ to do good works as a result of their salvation, not in order to gain it. Empower them to relentlessly pursue the good works you have prepared for them to accomplish. For your glory and their good, in the precious name of Christ, amen.

Write down any thoughts or ideas you may want to *Share*:

Day Two: Wisdom

Father, open my eyes so that I might *see* you more clearly, *savor* you more fully, and *share* you more freely.

Circle or underline any key words or phrases you *See*:

And he said to man, "Behold, the fear of the Lord, that is wisdom, and to turn away from evil is understanding." (Job 28:28)

The fear of the Lord is the beginning of wisdom; all those who practice it have a good understanding. His praise endures forever! (Psalm 111:10)

Savor these truths in prayer for you and your student:

Father, you are wise and wonderful in all you are and do. To fear you is to see you and ourselves accurately. Fearing you requires respect, honor, adoration, and humility because of your greatness and our dependence on you for all things. I pray that _____ would fear you and gain clearer vision every day to see you as you really are. Remove the obstacles that blind and deceive them from recognizing your work in this world. Make their hearts overflow with praise and thankfulness for all your sustaining goodness in their lives. Empower them through your wisdom to turn away from evil and take no delight in it. Strengthen them in their ability to help others see your greatness. For your glory and their good, in Jesus' all-wise and wonderful name, amen.

Write down any thoughts or ideas you may want to *Share*:

Day Three: Love

Father, open my eyes so that I might *see* you more clearly, *savor* you more fully, and *share* you more freely.

Circle or underline any key words or phrases you *See*:

And he said to him, "You shall love the Lord your God with all your heart and with all your soul and with all your mind. This is the great and first commandment. And a second is like it: You shall love your neighbor as yourself. On these two commandments depend all the Law and the Prophets." (Matthew 22:37-40)

Savor these truths in prayer for you and your student:

Father, thank you that your greatest command is for our greatest good. I pray that _____ would seek to love you with all of their heart, soul, and mind. Cause them to find their greatest delight in you. Give them understanding that their deepest desires can only be satisfied by loving you in all they say, think, and do. Do not let them grow weary in their pursuit to love you supremely. Protect them from the temptation to settle for lesser loves. Capture them with the magnificence of your love for them and cause them to be tenacious in loving others as themselves. Let their lives be a constant demonstration of your love to the world. For your glory and their good, in the wonderful name of Jesus, amen.

Write down any thoughts or ideas you may want to *Share*:

Day Four: Faith

Father, open my eyes so that I might *see* you more clearly, *savor* you more fully, and *share* you more freely.

Circle or underline any key words or phrases you *See*:

I know that you can do all things, and that no purpose of yours can be thwarted. (Job 42:2)

Ah, Lord GOD! It is you who have made the heavens and the earth by your great power and by your outstretched arm! Nothing is too hard for you... "Behold, I am the LORD, the God of all flesh. Is anything too hard for me?" (Jeremiah 32:17, 27)

Savor these truths in prayer for you and your student:

Father, every day we are confronted by limitations that tell us we are not enough, but it is empowering to know that you are more than enough. I pray for _____ today, that you would give them faith in your ability to do all things. Help them to believe that there is no purpose of yours that can be thwarted. Cause their hearts and minds to be in sync with your purposes in this world. When they are faced with impossible challenges, remind them that nothing is too hard for you. Cause them to know your greatest purpose for their lives: that you work out every circumstance for the good of those who love you, so that they might be conformed into the image of your Son. May you be praised forever! In Jesus' name, amen.

Write down any thoughts or ideas you may want to *Share*:

Day Five: Purity

Father, open my eyes so that I might *see* you more clearly, *savor* you more fully, and *share* you more freely.

Circle or underline any key words or phrases you *See*:

I have made a covenant with my eyes; how then could I gaze at a virgin? (Job 31:1)

Sheol and Abaddon are never satisfied, and never satisfied are the eyes of man. (Proverbs 27:20)

Savor these truths in prayer for you and your student:

Father, as I pray for _____ and their purity today, I ask that you would make them alert to the people, places, and things that they look upon. Help them to be like Job and make a covenant with their eyes, guarding their gaze and not looking at others inappropriately. Help them to diligently seek purity. Help them to understand that their purity can be fueled or foiled by the direction of their gaze. Protect them from the futility of trying to be satisfied by what they see. The eyes of man cannot be satisfied apart from you. You alone can create in them a satisfaction that supersedes all other lures or lusts that come before their eyes. For your glory and their good, in Jesus' name, amen.

Write down any thoughts or ideas you may want to *Share*:

Day Six: Speech

Father, open my eyes so that I might *see* you more clearly, *savor* you more fully, and *share* you more freely.

Circle or underline any key words or phrases you *See*:

One generation shall commend your works to another, and shall declare your mighty acts. On the glorious splendor of your majesty, and on your wondrous works, I will meditate. They shall speak of the might of your awesome deeds, and I will declare your greatness. (Psalm 145:4-6)

Savor these truths in prayer for you and your student:

> Father, thank you that there is no end to the greatness and wonder of your works. The might and majesty of your awesome deeds must be declared from one generation to another. I pray today that you would bring adult believers into _____ 's lives who have seen, savored, and are compelled to share your greatness with them. Give these adults courage to care and share. Cause them to take initiative to share the wondrous works that you have done in their lives. Cause your relentless hope to be established in their hearts as they hear stories of your great goodness. For your glory and their good, in Jesus' name, amen.

Write down any thoughts or ideas you may want to *Share*:

Day Seven: Conduct

Father, open my eyes so that I might *see* you more clearly, *savor* you more fully, and *share* you more freely.

Circle or underline any key words or phrases you *See*:

"This Book of the Law shall not depart from your mouth, but you shall meditate on it day and night, so that you may be careful to do according to all that is written in it. For then you will make your way prosperous, and then you will have good success. Have I not commanded you? Be strong and courageous. Do not be frightened, and do not be dismayed, for the LORD your God is with you wherever you go." (Joshua 1:8-9)

Savor these truths in prayer for you and your student:

Father, I praise you and thank you for the promises in your Word. I pray that _____ would take hold of your Word with all their hearts and minds. Give them joy in meditating on it day and night. Cause them to be quick to obey all that you command, knowing your promises of goodness will follow. Create in them a courageous and strong resolve to pursue all that you desire for them. Don't let fear cause them to falter. Fill them with faith to believe they can go anywhere you command. Cause the power of your presence to strengthen them to pursue your purposes with courage. For your glory and their good, in Jesus' name, amen.

Write down any thoughts or ideas you may want to *Share*:

Notes

CONGRATULATIONS!

You've made it through your first two weeks of prayer! I hope you're enjoying the journey so far. Your prayers are making a lasting impact on the next generation.

The Pray for Me Campaign team would love to hear how it's going so far! Connect with us on social media to share your story of what God is doing and read stories from other Prayer Champions and students. You can also email us or chat with us on our website. We can't wait to hear from you!

www.prayformecampaign.com
info@theyouthnetwork.org

The Pray for Me Campaign

pfmcampaign

pfmcampaign

WEEK THREE

The 7 Essentials in 7 Days

Grant me, O Lord my God, a mind to know you, a heart to seek you, wisdom to find you, conduct pleasing to you, faithful perseverance in waiting for you, and a hope of finally embracing you. Amen. — ST. THOMAS AQUINAS

...a spiritual life without prayer is like the gospel without Christ. — HENRI J.M. NOUWEN

Prayer is an act of brave trust in God. — RHONDA SOUDER

Day One: Favor

Father, open my eyes so that I might *see* you more clearly, *savor* you more fully, and *share* you more freely.

Circle or underline any key words or phrases you *See*:

Let not steadfast love and faithfulness forsake you; bind them around your neck; write them on the tablet of your heart. So you will find favor and good success in the sight of God and man. (Proverbs 3:3-4)

Savor these truths in prayer for you and your student:

Father, I pray for _____, that you would give them your special favor today. Cause your steadfast love and faithfulness to well up inside of them, strengthening their confidence in you. Give them minds and hearts for love and faithfulness that would transform their lives as well as the lives of those they touch. May their lives be so clearly marked by your love and faithfulness that favor and success would be their constant companions. Cause them to feel your hand of favor on their lives and remind them that where they go the favor of God goes. For your glory and their good, in Jesus' name, amen.

Write down any thoughts or ideas you may want to *Share*:

Day Two: Wisdom

Father, open my eyes so that I might *see* you more clearly, *savor* you more fully, and *share* you more freely.

Circle or underline any key words or phrases you *See:*

For the LORD gives wisdom; from his mouth come knowledge and under-standing; he stores up sound wisdom for the upright... (Proverbs 2:6-7)

Blessed is the one who finds wisdom, and the one who gets understanding... (Proverbs 3:13)

Savor these truths in prayer for you and your student:

Father, I pray that you would create in _____ a longing for you and your wisdom. I pray that you would give them eyes to see, ears to hear, and hearts to understand the wisdom found in your Word! Help them to embrace the truth of how limited their knowledge and understanding really is, and cause them to treasure the truth of your wisdom. Grant that they would be relentless in their pursuit of your wisdom, knowing that you bless those who find it. Bless them as they taste the sweetness of your wisdom. Create in them a deep understanding about life, which enables them to be a fountain of wise counsel to their friends. Make sharing about you and your wisdom as natural as breathing. For your glory and their good, in Jesus' name, amen.

Write down any thoughts or ideas you may want to *Share:*

Day Three: Love

Father, open my eyes so that I might *see* you more clearly, *savor* you more fully, and *share* you more freely.

Circle or underline any key words or phrases you *See*:

For as high as the heavens are above the earth, so great is his steadfast love toward those who fear him; as far as the east is from the west, so far does he remove our transgressions from us. (Psalm 103:11-12)

Savor these truths in prayer for you and your student:

Father, your love is great toward those who fear you! I pray that _____ would fear you. Create in them awe and respect for you that is unquenchable. Cause them to feel the fullness of your love for them that stretches to the highest heavens. Make the magnitude of your love the dominant force of their lives. Thank you that your forgiveness is perfect and complete. Let them feel the freedom of your complete and unending forgiveness through Jesus and his sacrifice every single day. For your glory and their good, in Jesus' name, amen.

Write down any thoughts or ideas you may want to *Share*:

Day Four: Faith

Father, open my eyes so that I might *see* you more clearly, *savor* you more fully, and *share* you more freely.

Circle or underline any key words or phrases you *See*:

And those who know your name put their trust in you, for you, O LORD, have not forsaken those who seek you. (Psalm 9:10)

Some trust in chariots and some in horses, but we trust in the name of the LORD our God. (Psalm 20:7)

Savor these truths in prayer for you and your student:

Father, your promises are true. You are faithful to those who put their trust in you! I pray for _____, that they would know your character, causing their hearts to grow large with faith and trust in you. Create in them confidence that your name represents all of your authority, power, and greatness. Help them to savor you as their Creator, Sustainer, Provider, Healer, and Redeemer. Take hold of them in such a way that they will passionately seek you, knowing that you will never forsake them. You are the Prince of Peace, so anoint them with your perfect peace. You are the King of Kings, so reign over them in all of your goodness. You are the Great I Am, so give them faith to trust you for all they need. For your glory and their good, in Jesus' name, amen.

Write down any thoughts or ideas you may want to *Share*:

Day Five: Purity

Father, open my eyes so that I might *see* you more clearly, *savor* you more fully, and *share* you more freely.

Circle or underline any key words or phrases you *See*:

Blessed are the pure in heart, for they shall see God.
(Matthew 5:8)

Savor these truths in prayer for you and your student:

Father, thank you for this day that you have ordained for
_____. I pray for their happiness today. Jesus said that
blessed are the pure in heart for they shall see God. Give them
uncontainable joy in you. Don't let them miss the wonder and
joy of seeing you because they settled for some false promise
of pleasure elsewhere. Give them a magnificent vision of your
greatness so that those empty promises would be powerless in
their hearts. It is by your Spirit that they are empowered to
walk in purity. Fill them with your Spirit today. Cause the joy
from seeing your magnificence to overflow in blessing and
purity to those around them. For your glory and their good,
in Jesus' name, amen.

Write down any thoughts or ideas you may want to *Share*:

Day Six: Speech

Father, open my eyes so that I might *see* you more clearly, *savor* you more fully, and *share* you more freely.

Circle or underline any key words or phrases you *See*:

When words are many, transgression is not lacking, but whoever restrains his lips is prudent. (Proverbs 10:19)

There is one whose rash words are like sword thrusts, but the tongue of the wise brings healing. Truthful lips endure forever, but a lying tongue is but for a moment. (Proverbs 12:18-19)

Savor these truths in prayer for you and your student:

Father, thank you for giving us the gift of language and the ability to express ourselves with words. It is through your wisdom and favor that we can use our words well. I pray that you would bless _____ with wisdom when they speak. Cause their words to be filled with wisdom from above, bringing healing everywhere they go. Help them to refrain from uttering rash words that damage and destroy. May their lips always speak the truth in love. Remind them that a lying tongue always comes to an undesirable end. Cause them to be wise with their words today for your glory and their good. In Jesus' name, amen.

Write down any thoughts or ideas you may want to *Share*:

Day Seven: Conduct

Father, open my eyes so that I might *see* you more clearly, *savor* you more fully, and *share* you more freely.

Circle or underline any key words or phrases you *See*:

Good and upright is the LORD; therefore he instructs sinners in the way. He leads the humble in what is right, and teaches the humble his way. All the paths of the LORD are steadfast love and faithfulness, for those who keep his covenant and his testimonies. (Psalm 25:8-10)

Savor these truths in prayer for you and your student:

Father, thank you that you are good and upright in all you do. You correct us in our sin and instruct us in the way we should go. I pray that you would create in _____ humble hearts. Empower them to follow your lead in all things. Cause them to be teachable and responsive to all of your purposes. Help them to pursue your path of steadfast love and faithfulness. Cause them to resist living out of pride, knowing that you give grace to the humble. Make your truth their treasure. For your glory and their good, in Jesus' name, amen.

Write down any thoughts or ideas you may want to *Share*:

Notes

The 7 Essentials in 7 Days

My daughter jokes about how she loves to run short distances at a long distance pace. I laugh every time she says it because I identify with it so much. I wonder if we could benefit by applying my daughter's running approach to our prayers. Here is what I mean: Even though they are short prayers, it doesn't mean you should speed through them. Pace yourself. You can even think of it as a prayer stroll. As you are praying, find a word, phrase, or sentence and linger over it for a little while. Don't feel the need to rush to the next sentence. Let God help you savor the elements of each passage and prayer long into the day. Enjoy your stroll.

Day One: Favor

Father, open my eyes so that I might *see* you more clearly, *savor* you more fully, and *share* you more freely.

Circle or underline any key words or phrases you *See*:

...since he himself gives to all mankind life and breath and every-thing... "in him we live and move and have our being." (Acts 17:25, 28)

What do you have that you did not receive? If then you received it, why do you boast as if you did not receive it? (1 Corinthians 4:7)

Savor these truths in prayer for you and your student:

Father, every breath is a gift of your grace and favor. It is from your hand that _____ have life and breath and all things today. It is in you that they live and move and have their being. Keep them from taking your constant sustaining goodness for granted. Create genuine delight in their hearts today for each breath. Give them eyes to see the wonder of your sustaining favor, and cause their hearts to be full with thanksgiving. For your glory and their good, in the all-sustaining name of Jesus, amen.

Write down any thoughts or ideas you may want to *Share*:

Day Two: Wisdom

Father, open my eyes so that I might *see* you more clearly, *savor* you more fully, and *share* you more freely.

Circle or underline any key words or phrases you *See*:

The words of the wise are like goads, and like nails firmly fixed are the col-lected sayings; they are given by one Shepherd. My son, beware of anything beyond these. Of making many books there is no end, and much study is a wea-riness of the flesh. The end of the matter; all has been heard. Fear God and keep his commandments, for this is the whole duty of man. For God will bring every deed into judgment, with every secret thing, whether good or evil. (Ecclesiastes 12:11-14)

Savor these truths in prayer for you and your student:

Father, thank you for providing this insightful summary of the power of Scriptural proverbs and reminding us that wis-dom comes from you, the Great Shepherd. I pray that _____ would look to you for their wisdom first and fore-most. Give them discernment in deciding where and how they will pursue wisdom. Help them wade into the Biblical proverbs, letting the words soak deeply into their lives. Strengthen them by the power of your Spirit to honor and obey you, knowing they're ultimately accountable to you. For your glory and their good, in Jesus' name, amen.

Write down any thoughts or ideas you may want to *Share*:

Day Three: Love

Father, open my eyes so that I might *see* you more clearly, *savor* you more fully, and *share* you more freely.

Circle or underline any key words or phrases you *See*:

For the love of money is a root of all kinds of evils. It is through this craving that some have wandered away from the faith and pierced themselves with many pangs. (1 Timothy 6:10)

Keep your life free from love of money, and be content with what you have, for he has said, "I will never leave you nor forsake you." So we can confidently say, "The Lord is my helper; I will not fear; what can man do to me?" (Hebrews 13:5-6)

Savor these truths in prayer for you and your student:

Father, as I pray for _____ today, I long for them to have their hearts captured by you and your love. So many things can steal their affections—the love of money being one of the most significant and potentially tragic. Your Word says that the love of money is the root of all kinds of evils. Don't let that ever be the driving force of their lives. May your glory and the good of others be their primary goal. Protect them from fear of the unknown, which can tempt them to rely on money. Give them confidence in knowing that you will never leave or forsake them. You are their helper; there is no need to fear. For your glory and their good, in Jesus' name, amen.

Write down any thoughts or ideas you may want to *Share*:

Day Four: Faith

Father, open my eyes so that I might *see* you more clearly, *savor* you more fully, and *share* you more freely.

Circle or underline any key words or phrases you *See*:

The fear of man lays a snare, but whoever trusts in the Lord is safe. (Proverbs 29:25)

Savor these truths in prayer for you and your student:

Father, I pray that you would help _____ to not fear man. Fearing man creates a snare in our hearts and minds. Set them free from those snares and difficulties that come from giving man too big of a place in our hearts and minds. Cause them to trust in you so that you would be at the forefront of their hearts and minds. You are safe and good, and you alone can set them free from the fear of man. Reign in what they think, say, and do today. For your glory and their good, in Jesus' name, amen.

Write down any thoughts or ideas you may want to *Share*:

Day Five: Purity

Father, open my eyes so that I might *see* you more clearly, *savor* you more fully, and *share* you more freely.

Circle or underline any key words or phrases you *See*:

Keep your heart with all vigilance, for from it flow the springs of life. (Proverbs 4:23)

And he said, "What comes out of a person is what defiles him. For from within, out of the heart of man, come evil thoughts, sexual immorality, theft, murder, adultery, coveting, wickedness, deceit, sensuality, envy, slander, pride, foolishness. All these evil things come from within, and they defile a person." (Mark 7:20-23)

Savor these truths in prayer for you and your student:

Father, in our pursuit of following you in faithfulness and becoming like you in holiness, we realize that some actions are more important than others. Guarding our hearts is one of those vital acts. I pray that _____ would exercise vigilance in guarding their heart by the power of your Spirit. Help them to see the places where they need to protect their heart better. Help them to find friends that will strengthen their resolve to guard their hearts. Cause them to see with clarity the disappointing consequences of people who live with unguarded hearts. Fill them with your Spirit so that rivers of living water will flow out of them. For your glory and their good, in Jesus' name, amen.

Write down any thoughts or ideas you may want to *Share*:

Day Six: Speech

Father, open my eyes so that I might *see* you more clearly, *savor* you more fully, and *share* you more freely.

Circle or underline any key words or phrases you *See*:

A soft answer turns away wrath, but a harsh word stirs up anger. The tongue of the wise commends knowledge, but the mouths of fools pour out folly...A gentle tongue is a tree of life, but perverseness in it breaks the spirit. (Proverbs 15:1-2, 4)

Savor these truths in prayer for you and your student:

Father, thank you for the power of soft and gentle speech. I pray that you would provide _____ with people who would lavish them with the goodness of soft and gentle speech. In the same way I pray that they would be generous in offering up words that are soft and gentle to others. Cause the fruit of their words to be a tree of life, turning away wrath and anger. Let wisdom flow from their lips, commending knowledge that is life-giving to all who hear. Protect them from giving or receiving harsh words that stir up anger or hate. Give them the ability to graciously change the subject when perverse speech breaks out around them. Do not let evil and harsh words be used to harm them in any way. Help them to embrace your truth so they can overcome any false words directed toward them. For your glory and their good, in Jesus' name, amen.

Write down any thoughts or ideas you may want to *Share*:

Day Seven: Conduct

Father, open my eyes so that I might *see* you more clearly, *savor* you more fully, and *share* you more freely.

Circle or underline any key words or phrases you *See*:

Be appalled, O heavens, at this; be shocked, be utterly desolate, declares the LORD, for my people have committed two evils: they have forsaken me, the fountain of living waters, and hewed out cisterns for themselves, broken cisterns that can hold no water. (Jeremiah 2:12-13)

Savor these truths in prayer for you and your student:

Father, thank you that you are the fountain of living waters and the only place we can be perfectly satisfied. I pray that _____ would believe with all of their hearts that you are their ultimate source of complete satisfaction. Make them alert to even the subtle tendencies to turn away from you to find happiness somewhere else. Cause them to see and understand the weight of loss and desolation that comes from turning away from you. Help them to flee the futility of trying to find happiness through their own devices. Forgive them when they engage or pursue you in a casual way. Create in them a craving for you and your ways in all things. Strengthen them to help those around them turn away from their futile ways and find fullness of joy in you. For your glory and their good, in Jesus' name, amen.

Write down any thoughts or ideas you may want to *Share*:

Notes

WEEK FIVE

Favor

To be grateful is to recognize the Love of God in everything He has given us—and He has given us everything. Every breath we draw is a gift of His Love, every moment of existence is a grace, for it brings with it immense graces from Him. — DON POSTEMA

And whatever you do, in word or deed, do everything in the name of the Lord Jesus, giving thanks to God the Father through him. (Colossians 3:17)

...pray without ceasing, give thanks in all circumstances; for this is the will of God in Christ Jesus for you. (1 Thessalonians 5:17-18)

Day One of Favor

Father, open my eyes so that I might *see* you more clearly, *savor* you more fully, and *share* you more freely.

Circle or underline any key words or phrases you *See*:

For I am the least of the apostles, unworthy to be called an apostle, because I persecuted the church of God. But by the grace of God I am what I am, and his grace toward me was not in vain. On the contrary, I worked harder than any of them, though it was not I, but the grace of God that is with me. (1 Corinthians 15:9-10)

Savor these truths in prayer for you and your student:

Father, your grace and favor are beyond understanding, and yet I pray that _____ would see and savor it for all it is worth. Don't let them think for a moment that your grace is a passive thing, but allow them to see that your grace is a mighty force that empowers them to work harder at pursuing your purposes. Instill in them the truth that it is your grace working behind the scenes to create goodness in their lives and the world. Create in them a longing for your grace. Cause them to relentlessly pursue your grace through prayer. For your glory and their good, in the gracious name of Jesus, amen.

Write down any thoughts or ideas you may want to *Share*:

Day Two of Favor

Father, open my eyes so that I might *see* you more clearly, *savor* you more fully, and *share* you more freely.

Circle or underline any key words or phrases you *See*:

Satisfy us in the morning with your steadfast love, that we may rejoice and be glad all our days. (Psalm 90:14)

Savor these truths in prayer for you and your student:

Father, every day _____ will be presented with things that promise to make them happy and satisfy the longings of their heart. You alone can satisfy their hearts and make them glad all their days. I pray that you will satisfy them early and often with your steadfast love. Don't let them be deceived by the lure of empty promises offered by the world. Give them eyes to see your steadfast love all through the day. Awaken the taste buds of their heart to tenaciously savor the sweetness of your love every time they see it. Cause them to share their satisfaction in your steadfast love freely as they live for you each day. For your glory and their good, in the all-satisfying name of Jesus, amen.

Write down any thoughts or ideas you may want to *Share*:

Day Three of Favor

Father, open my eyes so that I might *see* you more clearly, *savor* you more fully, and *share* you more freely.

Circle or underline any key words or phrases you *See*:

"Glory to God in the highest, and on earth peace among those with whom he is pleased!" (Luke 2:14)

Now may the Lord of peace himself give you peace at all times in every way. The Lord be with you all. (2 Thessalonians 3:16)

Savor these truths in prayer for you and your student:

Father, when your angels entered our world, they declared glory to you and peace to us—specifically, peace to those with whom you are pleased and on whom your favor rests. Cause your favor to rest on _____ today, and may they know your peace that surpasses all understanding. Grant that those with any restlessness in their hearts would be surrendered to you, that you would reign with your peace. Create in them a longing for the peace that you offer to the world through Jesus. Help them to know that your peace in Jesus brings freedom that the world does not know. For your glory and their good, in the name of the Prince of Peace, Jesus, amen.

Write down any thoughts or ideas you may want to *Share*:

Day Four of Favor

Father, open my eyes so that I might *see* you more clearly, *savor* you more fully, and *share* you more freely.

Circle or underline any key words or phrases you *See*:

What then shall we say to these things? If God is for us, who can be against us? He who did not spare his own Son but gave him up for us all, how will he not also with him graciously give us all things? (Romans 8:31-32)

Savor these truths in prayer for you and your student:

Father, I pray today that _____ would sense the magnitude of your goodness toward them. Don't let them miss the wonder of what you have done for them in Jesus. Allow their hearts and minds to be amazed by your generous love. Cause them to seek the favor of your presence, protection, and provision in all of life. Remind them that all the resources of heaven are for them in Jesus. Father, there is nothing greater you could have given or provided than the sacrifice of your Son. Let the significance of Jesus' life, death, and resurrection sink into the depths of their hearts. Create in them a relentless confidence in God because of the truths of Romans 8:31-32. For your glory and their good, in Jesus' name, amen.

Write down any thoughts or ideas you may want to *Share*:

Day Five of Favor

Father, open my eyes so that I might *see* you more clearly, *savor* you more fully, and *share* you more freely.

Circle or underline any key words or phrases you *See*:

Let the favor of the Lord our God be upon us, and establish the work of our hands upon us; yes, establish the work of our hands! (Psalm 90:17)

Savor these truths in prayer for you and your student:

Father, I pray for _____ today, that they would know your favor in their work. Help them to realize that whatever they set their hands to do should be done to your glory. You have created them for good works and they should devote themselves fully to what you have called them to at this point in their lives. Establish the work of their hands. Make it clear that your hand of favor is upon them through your provision, protection, presence, and purposes. Give them joy in their work, and make them a joy to work with. Cause them to study with diligence and to delight in the truths that they are able to learn. For your glory and their good, in Jesus' name, amen.

Write down any thoughts or ideas you may want to *Share*:

Day Six of Favor

Father, open my eyes so that I might *see* you more clearly, *savor* you more fully, and *share* you more freely.

Circle or underline any key words or phrases you *See*:

It is he who remembered us in our low estate, for his steadfast love endures forever; and rescued us from our foes, for his steadfast love endures forever; he who gives food to all flesh, for his steadfast love endures forever. Give thanks to the God of heaven, for his steadfast love endures forever. (Psalm 136:23-26)

Savor these truths in prayer for you and your student:

Father, your steadfast love for _____ endures forever. It is through your grace and favor that they are able to know and experience your steadfast love toward them. In whatever way they may be discouraged today, remember them and cause them to have hope. Grant them discernment concerning anyone who would seek to do them harm. Guard and protect them. Give them eyes to see your provision, and stir up within them relentless thankfulness toward you. For your glory and their good, in the matchless name of Jesus, amen.

Write down any thoughts or ideas you may want to *Share*:

Day Seven of Favor

Father, open my eyes so that I might *see* you more clearly, *savor* you more fully, and *share* you more freely.

Circle or underline any key words or phrases you *See*:

He [Jesus] is the image of the invisible God, the firstborn of all creation. For by him all things were created, in heaven and on earth, visible and invisible, whether thrones or dominions or rulers or authorities—all things were created through him and for him. And he is before all things, and in him all things hold together. (Colossians 1:15-17)

Savor these truths in prayer for you and your student:

Father, the message in this passage is clear: all of life is about Jesus. Your words declare that everything owes its existence and sustenance to Jesus. Not only were all things created through him, they were created *for* him. Give _____ understanding and insight that Jesus is the center of all things. Create in their hearts and minds a delight in you that is uncontainable. Cause this delight never to cease, so that each day would be filled with tasting, seeing, and delighting in all that Jesus is. For your glory and their good, in the matchless name of King Jesus, amen.

Write down any thoughts or ideas you may want to *Share*:

Notes

Wisdom

One of the beautiful aspects of prayer is that it is not just one directional. It is not just a cathartic experience where we unload on God to feel better. God communicates to us when we pray if we pause long enough to listen. God uses his Word and his Spirit to bring guidance, understanding, and conviction. You can be sure that he will never bring something to mind that is contrary to his Word. So ask him for guidance, understanding, and even conviction concerning anything in your world that needs to be addressed. Don't be afraid—he wants the best for you.

Search me, O God, and know my heart! Try me and know my thoughts! And see if there be any grievous way in me, and lead me in the way everlasting! (Psalm 139:23-24)

Day One of Wisdom

Father, open my eyes so that I might *see* you more clearly, *savor* you more fully, and *share* you more freely.

Circle or underline any key words or phrases you *See*:

Thus says the LORD: "Let not the wise man boast in his wisdom, let not the mighty man boast in his might, let not the rich man boast in his riches, but let him who boasts boast in this, that he understands and knows me, that I am the LORD who practices steadfast love, justice, and righteousness in the earth. For in these things I delight, declares the LORD." (Jeremiah 9:23-24)

Savor these truths in prayer for you and your student:

Father, I pray today that _____ would not boast or find their identity in their own wisdom. Protect them from the lure of feeling that their wisdom makes them superior to other people. Let their identity be found in you. Give them eyes to see where your love, justice, and righteousness are needed. Give them resolve to apply your wisdom to these situations whole-heartedly, even when it is hard. For your glory and their good, in Jesus' name, amen.

Write down any thoughts or ideas you may want to *Share*:

Day Two of Wisdom

Father, open my eyes so that I might *see* you more clearly, *savor* you more fully, and *share* you more freely.

Circle or underline any key words or phrases you *See*:

Let no one deceive himself. If anyone among you thinks that he is wise in this age, let him become a fool that he may become wise. For the wisdom of this world is folly with God. For it is written, "He catches the wise in their craftiness," and again, "The Lord knows the thoughts of the wise, that they are futile." So let no one boast in men. For all things are yours, whether Paul or Apollos or Cephas or the world or life or death or the present or the future—all are yours, and you are Christ's, and Christ is God's. (1 Corinthians 3:18-23)

Savor these truths in prayer for you and your student:

Father, it is so easy to be deceived into thinking that the ways of this world are wise. I pray that you would protect _____ from this deception. Give them confidence in you that supersedes their confidence in man. Help them turn to you in complete reliance, knowing that all things are yours and therefore their boast should be in you. Give them great pleasure in you as the source of all truth. For your glory and their good, in the supreme name of Christ, amen.

Write down any thoughts or ideas you may want to *Share*:

Day Three of Wisdom

Father, open my eyes so that I might *see* you more clearly, *savor* you more fully, and *share* you more freely.

Circle or underline any key words or phrases you *See*:

I do not cease to give thanks for you, remembering you in my prayers, that the God of our Lord Jesus Christ, the Father of glory, may give you the Spirit of wisdom and of revelation in the knowledge of him, having the eyes of your hearts enlightened, that you may know what is the hope to which he has called you, what are the riches of his glorious inheritance in the saints, and what is the immeasurable greatness of his power toward us who believe, according to the working of his great might that he worked in Christ when he raised him from the dead... (Ephesians 1:16-20)

Savor these truths in prayer for you and your student:

Father, I pray that you would give _____ your Spirit of wisdom, revelation, and knowledge. Enlighten the eyes of their hearts so that they might receive all the goodness that comes from each of these gifts. Cause them to have hope and purpose to see the wonder of the inheritance you have in store for them. Cause them to find rest and strength in the immeasurable greatness of your power—the same power that raised Jesus from the dead. Don't let them settle for living a life that is not fueled by your Spirit. For your glory and their good, in Jesus' name, amen.

Write down any thoughts or ideas you may want to *Share*:

Day Four of Wisdom

Father, open my eyes so that I might *see* you more clearly, *savor* you more fully, and *share* you more freely.

Circle or underline any key words or phrases you *See*:

Walk in wisdom toward outsiders, making the best use of the time. (Colossians 4:5)

Look carefully then how you walk, not as unwise but as wise, making the best use of the time, because the days are evil. Therefore do not be foolish, but understand what the will of the Lord is. And do not get drunk with wine, for that is debauchery, but be filled with the Spirit... (Ephesians 5:15-18)

Savor these truths in prayer for you and your student:

Father, I pray for _____, that they would live carefully. Cause them to know that every decision leads to a destination. Help them to be persistent in turning away from evil. When they are weak, bring strong friends into their lives to help hold them accountable. Remind them that they were made to reflect your greatness to the world. Give them resolve to pursue righteousness every day. Your Word is the sword of the Spirit that is able to cut through the lies of this world. Give them a relentless desire to drink deeply of your Word every day so that they will be filled with your Spirit. For your glory and their good, in Jesus' name, amen.

Write down any thoughts or ideas you may want to *Share*:

Day Five of Wisdom

Father, open my eyes so that I might *see* you more clearly, *savor* you more fully, and *share* you more freely.

Circle or underline any key words or phrases you *See*:

And it is my prayer that your love may abound more and more, with knowledge and all discernment, so that you may approve what is excellent, and so be pure and blameless for the day of Christ, filled with the fruit of righteousness that comes through Jesus Christ, to the glory and praise of God. (Philippians 1:9-11)

Savor these truths in prayer for you and your student:

Father, I pray the words of the apostle Paul for _____ today. Cause their love for you to flourish, thus deepening their discernment of what is right and wrong. As their love for you deepens, help them to better understand your love for them. Empower them to live lives that demonstrate what is excellent, pure, and blameless. Produce in them the fruit of righteousness that directly results from the power of your Spirit. For your glory and their good, in Jesus' name, amen.

Write down any thoughts or ideas you may want to *Share*:

Day Six of Wisdom

Father, open my eyes so that I might *see* you more clearly, *savor* you more fully, and *share* you more freely.

Circle or underline any key words or phrases you *See*:

But as for you, continue in what you have learned and have firmly believed, knowing from whom you learned it and how from childhood you have been acquainted with the sacred writings, which are able to make you wise for salvation through faith in Christ Jesus. All Scripture is breathed out by God and profitable for teaching, for reproof, for correction, and for training in righteousness, that the man of God may be complete, equipped for every good work. (2 Timothy 3:14-17)

Savor these truths in prayer for you and your student:

Father, there is nothing more important than knowing you personally. Give _____ wisdom as they pursue a deep and life-giving relationship with you through your Word. Don't let them be deceived by the lies of this world; assure them that Jesus is the only way by which they can be saved and made right with you. Create in them teachable hearts and minds so that they may receive the full benefits of engaging with your Word. Cause them to flourish in freely sharing the truths of your Word. For your glory and their good, in Jesus' name, amen.

Write down any thoughts or ideas you may want to *Share*:

Day Seven of Wisdom

Father, open my eyes so that I might *see* you more clearly, *savor* you more fully, and *share* you more freely.

Circle or underline any key words or phrases you *See*:

Who is wise and understanding among you? By his good conduct let him show his works in the meekness of wisdom...But the wisdom from above is first pure, then peaceable, gentle, open to reason, full of mercy and good fruits, impartial and sincere. And a harvest of righteousness is sown in peace by those who make peace. (James 3:13, 17-18)

Savor these truths in prayer for you and your student:

Father, wise people bear fruit that reveals their wisdom. I pray that _____ would have a hunger and thirst for your wisdom. Cause them to pursue it with diligent humility. Give them a keen ability to spot wisdom that is from you. Cause them to bear the fruit of wisdom that is pure, peaceful, gentle, open to reason, impartial, and sincere. Bring people into their lives who know and live out your wise purposes. May their lives produce a harvest of righteousness that is sown in peace. For your glory and their good, in the precious name of Jesus, amen.

Write down any thoughts or ideas you may want to *Share*:

Notes

WEEK SEVEN

Love

Give us, O Lord, a steadfast heart, which no unworthy affection may drag downwards; give us an unconquered heart, which no tribulation can wear out; give us an upright heart, which no unworthy purpose may tempt aside. Bestow upon us also, O Lord our God, understanding to know you, diligence to seek you, wisdom to find you, and a faithfulness that may finally embrace you; through Jesus Christ our Lord. — ST. THOMAS AQUINAS

Day One of Love

Father, open my eyes so that I might *see* you more clearly, *savor* you more fully, and *share* you more freely.

Circle or underline any key words or phrases you *See*:

Love is patient and kind; love does not envy or boast; it is not arrogant or rude. It does not insist on its own way; it is not irritable or resentful; it does not rejoice at wrongdoing, but rejoices with the truth. Love bears all things, believes all things, hopes all things, endures all things. Love never ends. As for prophecies, they will pass away; as for tongues, they will cease; as for knowledge, it will pass away. (1 Corinthians 13:4-8)

Savor these truths in prayer for you and your student:

Father, your love endures forever! I pray today that _____ would receive your love through other people. Grant that they would know your patience and feel your kindness throughout this day. Give them favor to encounter people filled with your love today. Cause them to be people of your love to others today, showing patience and kindness especially when they encounter people who are arrogant and rude. May they be the sweet aroma of Christ to people who insist on their own way. Cause your supernatural love to empower them to believe, hope, and endure all things. For your glory and their good, in Jesus' name, amen.

Write down any thoughts or ideas you may want to *Share*:

Day Two of Love

Father, open my eyes so that I might *see* you more clearly, *savor* you more fully, and *share* you more freely.

Circle or underline any key words or phrases you *See*:

A new commandment I give to you, that you love one another: just as I have loved you, you also are to love one another. By this all people will know that you are my disciples, if you have love for one another. (John 13:34-35)

Savor these truths in prayer for you and your student:

Father, I pray today for _____ that they would embrace your commandment to love one another. Give them eyes to see and hearts to understand how you have personally loved them. Cause them to comprehend just how deep, wide, long, and high your love is for them so that they can love others fully. Help them to love and obey your command to love one another with daily diligence so that the world will know that they belong to you. Protect them from believing that they can disregard loving others and still be seen as belonging to you. Your children love because you have loved them. For your glory and their good, in Jesus' name, amen.

Write down any thoughts or ideas you may want to *Share*:

Day Three of Love

Father, open my eyes so that I might *see* you more clearly, *savor* you more fully, and *share* you more freely.

Circle or underline any key words or phrases you *See*:

There is no fear in love, but perfect love casts out fear. For fear has to do with punishment, and whoever fears has not been perfected in love. We love because he first loved us. If anyone says, "I love God," and hates his brother, he is a liar; for he who does not love his brother whom he has seen cannot love God whom he has not seen. And this commandment we have from him: whoever loves God must also love his brother. (1 John 4:18-21)

Savor these truths in prayer for you and your student:

Father, give _____ eyes to see their fears and grant them the confidence that your perfect love is the answer to those fears. Cause them to run to you with each and every fear so that they may be swallowed up by your perfect love. I pray that they would know the full freedom of your love toward them in Jesus. Help them to understand that your love transforms how they love others. Where their love is weak, strengthen it. Make their hearts large in love toward you and man. Help them to savor the freedom that comes from your perfect love and cause them to relentlessly share your perfect love with others. For your glory and their good, in the loving name of Jesus, amen.

Write down any thoughts or ideas you may want to *Share*:

Day Four of Love

Father, open my eyes so that I might *see* you more clearly, *savor* you more fully, and *share* you more freely.

Circle or underline any key words or phrases you *See*:

In this the love of God was made manifest among us, that God sent his only Son into the world, so that we might live through him. In this is love, not that we have loved God but that he loved us and sent his Son to be the propitiation for our sins. Beloved, if God so loved us, we also ought to love one another. (1 John 4:9-11)

Savor these truths in prayer for you and your student:

Father, thank you for making your love clear in Jesus! Cause _____ to grasp the magnitude of your love in sending your Son into the world. Help them see that their sins have separated them from you, and you solved that separation through Jesus' sacrifice. Let them savor the sweetness of your sacrifice for their sins. Cause their hearts to be filled with lavish thankfulness because of your great love and provision. Grant that sacrificial love would be one of the distinguishing marks of their lives. Help them love one another the way that you have loved them in Jesus. Give them eyes to see how they can show your love to others today. For your glory and their good, in Jesus' name, amen.

Write down any thoughts or ideas you may want to *Share*:

Day Five of Love

Father, open my eyes so that I might *see* you more clearly, *savor* you more fully, and *share* you more freely.

Circle or underline any key words or phrases you *See*:

For God so loved the world, that he gave his only Son, that whoever believes in him should not perish but have eternal life. For God did not send his Son into the world to condemn the world, but in order that the world might be saved through him. Whoever believes in him is not condemned, but whoever does not believe is condemned already, because he has not believed in the name of the only Son of God. (John 3:16-18)

Savor these truths in prayer for you and your student:

Father, give _____ eyes to see the scope of your love for the world. Cause them to grasp your generous personal sacrifice that made eternal life possible by giving your Son, Jesus. Help their hearts to embrace the fact that Jesus came to save and not to condemn. Protect them from thinking that believing in Jesus doesn't matter. Don't let them shake off the magnitude and weight of the truth that rejecting the only Son of God results in condemnation. Give them a relentless desire to invite unbelievers to put their trust in Jesus alone for life, a life that starts now and lasts forever. For your glory and their good, in the saving name of Jesus, amen.

Write down any thoughts or ideas you may want to *Share*:

Day Six of Love

Father, open my eyes so that I might *see* you more clearly, *savor* you more fully, and *share* you more freely.

Circle or underline any key words or phrases you *See*:

Beloved, let us love one another, for love is from God, and whoever loves has been born of God and knows God. Anyone who does not love does not know God, because God is love. (1 John 4:7-8)

Savor these truths in prayer for you and your student:

Father, open the eyes of _____'s heart to see that love is from you. There is no other place that they can go to satisfy their hearts' desires apart from you and your love. Cause them to long for you and to drink deeply of your love. Grant that they would love others, knowing that whoever loves has been born of you and knows you. Keep them from minimizing the importance of being loving people. Don't let them shrug off or take lightly any tendency they have to hold a grudge, be bitter, or be disrespectful of others. Help them to embrace the truth that if we are not marked by a life of love, then in spite of what we say, we probably don't really know you, because you are love! For your glory and their good, in Jesus' name, amen.

Write down any thoughts or ideas you may want to *Share*:

Day Seven of Love

Father, open my eyes so that I might *see* you more clearly, *savor* you more fully, and *share* you more freely.

Circle or underline any key words or phrases you *See*:

For while we were still weak, at the right time Christ died for the ungodly. For one will scarcely die for a righteous person—though perhaps for a good person one would dare even to die—but God shows his love for us in that while we were still sinners, Christ died for us. (Romans 5:6-8)

Savor these truths in prayer for you and your student:

Father, thank you for revealing the magnificence of your love by redeeming those no one else would have even considered. Help _____ to see the magnitude of your sacrifice for them. Give them eyes to see how this exalts your greatness. Help their weak and feeble hearts to grasp the surpassing greatness of your provision. Stir within them thankfulness at every turn for redeeming them from the domain of darkness and establishing in them the kingdom of your beloved Son, Jesus. For your glory and their good, in the all-powerful name of Jesus Christ, amen.

Write down any thoughts or ideas you may want to *Share*:

Notes

Faith

Praying for your student by yourself is invigorating, but I want to encourage you to consider widening your circle. Find a friend who is also a Prayer Champion and pray together perhaps once a week. If that's too big a commitment for you, consider doing it once a month. You will find that praying this prayer guide with someone is easy and incredibly encouraging. You may find it so encouraging that you create a Prayer Champions' prayer group to strengthen your efforts of interceding for the next generation!

For where two or three are gathered in my name, there am I among them. (Matthew 18:20)

Day One of Faith

Father, open my eyes so that I might *see* you more clearly, *savor* you more fully, and *share* you more freely.

Circle or underline any key words or phrases you *See*:

And without faith it is impossible to please him, for whoever would draw near to God must believe that he exists and that he rewards those who seek him. (Hebrews 11:6)

Savor these truths in prayer for you and your student:

Father, without faith it is impossible to please you. I pray for _____ today, that you would give them an insatiable longing to please you, and that this longing would be met with a heart that is alive with faith. Create in them a diligent desire for closeness with you. Fuel their faith to trust in you daily in relationships and careers, hardships and pleasures. Be the object of their faith and may their reward be a heart that is satisfied with all that you are for them. For your glory and their good, in Jesus' name, amen.

Write down any thoughts or ideas you may want to *share*:

Day Two of Faith

Father, open my eyes so that I might *see* you more clearly, *savor* you more fully, and *share* you more freely.

Circle or underline any key words or phrases you *See*:

Therefore, since we are surrounded by so great a cloud of witnesses, let us also lay aside every weight, and sin which clings so closely, and let us run with endurance the race that is set before us, looking to Jesus, the founder and perfecter of our faith, who for the joy that was set before him endured the cross, despising the shame, and is seated at the right hand of the throne of God. (Hebrews 12:1-2)

Savor these truths in prayer for you and your student:

Father, you have called us to a race and it is not a sprint. I ask today that _____ would run with endurance. Don't let them get sidetracked when they run into difficulties. Inspire them with the testimonies of all those who have run before them. Cause them to let go of the things that hold them back. Free them from their sins and allow them to forgive those who sin against them. Give them a vision of you as the author and perfecter of their faith. Empower them with the strength to run the race. Give them joy in you that is so satisfying and powerful that it propels them forward in faith to do great things for your glory. May you be praised forever! In Jesus' name, amen.

Write down any thoughts or ideas you may want to *Share*:

Day Three of Faith

Father, open my eyes so that I might *see* you more clearly, *savor* you more fully, and *share* you more freely.

Circle or underline any key words or phrases you *See*:

You keep him in perfect peace whose mind is stayed on you, because he trusts in you. Trust in the LORD forever, for the LORD GOD is an everlasting rock. (Isaiah 26:3-4)

Savor these truths in prayer for you and your student:

Father, you provide perfect peace to those who keep you in the forefront of their minds. I pray that _____ would fix their minds on you today. Help them to see fear, worry, and anxiety as signals to turn to you, because freedom from these things can only be found in you. Let them understand that any peace they're experiencing is the result of trusting in you. Cause them to know that you are the Everlasting Rock, the only trustworthy source in which they can put their faith. May you be blessed forever, in Jesus' name, amen.

Write down any thoughts or ideas you may want to *Share*:

Day Four of Faith

Father, open my eyes so that I might *see* you more clearly, *savor* you more fully, and *share* you more freely.

Circle or underline any key words or phrases you *See*:

And Jesus said to him, "If you can! All things are possible for one who believes." Immediately the father of the child cried out and said, "I believe; help my unbelief!" (Mark 9:23-24)

Savor these truths in prayer for you and your student:

Father, thank you for the promises that you offer in your Word. Thank you for the hope that you offer to your children who trust you with their lives. I pray that you would give _____ eyes to see your promises. Help them to recognize whether they have faith or not. When they don't, cause them to call out to you in humility: "I believe! Help my unbelief!" Give them pleasure in offering a simple plea for more faith. Father, increase their faith! For your glory and their good, in the faithful name of Jesus, amen.

Write down any thoughts or ideas you may want to *Share*:

Day Five of Faith

Father, open my eyes so that I might *see* you more clearly, *savor* you more fully, and *share* you more freely.

Circle or underline any key words or phrases you *See*:

To this end we always pray for you, that our God may make you worthy of his calling and may fulfill every resolve for good and every work of faith by his power, so that the name of our Lord Jesus may be glorified in you, and you in him, according to the grace of our God and the Lord Jesus Christ. (2 Thessalonians 1:11-12)

Savor these truths in prayer for you and your student:

Father, I echo the apostle Paul's prayer as I pray for _____ today. May you make them worthy of your calling on their lives. Don't let them ever imagine that they are in this alone and can make themselves worthy apart from you. You alone make them worthy! Give them confidence that you are working in them today. By your great grace and favor I pray that you would establish and bring to fruition what you are stirring within them. Do all this so that your name would be glorified in them and the world would know that they are your precious and loved children. For your glory and their good, in Jesus' name, amen.

Write down any thoughts or ideas you may want to *Share*:

Day Six of Faith

Father, open my eyes so that I might *see* you more clearly, *savor* you more fully, and *share* you more freely.

Circle or underline any key words or phrases you *See*:

Fight the good fight of the faith. Take hold of the eternal life to which you were called and about which you made the good confession in the presence of many witnesses. (1 Timothy 6:12)

I have fought the good fight, I have finished the race, I have kept the faith. Henceforth there is laid up for me the crown of righteousness... (2 Timothy 4:7-8)

Savor these truths in prayer for you and your student:

Father, being your follower is a fight of faith to believe your good and perfect promises over the deceptive promises of the world, the flesh, and the devil. I pray that _____ would surrender their hearts to you and seek the power of your Spirit to believe all that you have promised. Remind them that winning this fight means abiding in you. Give them resolve to believe what you say in your Word. Cause their hearts to rejoice in the truth that you have prepared a place for them as their Savior, Redeemer, and King. May the promise of eternal life with you compel them to fight the good fight of faith. For your glory and their good. In Jesus' name, amen.

Write down any thoughts or ideas you may want to *Share*:

Day Seven of Faith

Father, open my eyes so that I might *see* you more clearly, *savor* you more fully, and *share* you more freely.

Circle or underline any key words or phrases you *See*:

...and I pray that the sharing of your faith may become effective for the full knowledge of every good thing that is in us for the sake of Christ. (Philemon 1:6)

Savor these truths in prayer for you and your student:

Father, your glory, steadfast love, and faithfulness are worthy of sharing at every opportunity. I pray today that _____ would be alert to all of your promises and the truth of your Word. Give them awareness of your steadfast love and faithfulness in their personal lives as well. Cause your faithfulness to be in the forefront of their hearts and minds. Give them the freedom to naturally share your greatness with those around them. As they share, establish in their hearts the full knowledge of every good thing that is theirs because of Christ. Grant them your favor as they speak on your behalf in this world. Soften the hearts of those who hear of your goodness through them. For your glory and their good, in Jesus' name, amen.

Write down any thoughts or ideas you may want to *Share*:

Notes

Purity

If we don't feel strong desires for the manifestation of the glory of God, it is not because we have drunk deeply and are satisfied. It is because we have nibbled so long at the table of the world. Our soul is stuffed with small things, and there is no room for the great. — JOHN PIPER

Day One of Purity

Father, open my eyes so that I might *see* you more clearly, *savor* you more fully, and *share* you more freely.

Circle or underline any key words or phrases you *See*:

No temptation has overtaken you that is not common to man. God is faithful, and he will not let you be tempted beyond your ability, but with the temptation he will also provide the way of escape, that you may be able to endure it. (1 Corinthians 10:13)

Savor these truths in prayer for you and your student:

Father, thank you for the reminder that the temptations that we face are common to all mankind. The enemy of our souls wants us to believe that we are alone in our sin and temptations, but you have assured us that this is not the case. I pray that _____ would know that their temptations are not unique to them. Help them to know that you will help them overcome their temptations. Give them faith to believe your promise that you will not allow them to be tempted beyond their ability. Don't let them forget that your promise of success is accompanied by a call to endure. Forge in them a faith that depends completely on the power of your Spirit. For your glory and their good, in Jesus' name, amen.

Write down any thoughts or ideas you may want to *Share*:

Day Two of Purity

Father, open my eyes so that I might *see* you more clearly, *savor* you more fully, and *share* you more freely.

Circle or underline any key words or phrases you *See*:

For this is the will of God, your sanctification: that you abstain from sexual immorality; that each one of you know how to control his body in holiness and honor, not in the passion of lust like the Gentiles who do not know God...For God has not called us for impurity, but in holiness. Therefore whoever disregards this, disregards not man but God, who gives his Holy Spirit to you. (1 Thessalonians 4:3-5, 7-8)

Savor these truths in prayer for you and your student:

Father, thank you for making your will for our lives known. It is your will that we be sanctified or made holy specifically in our sexual relationships. I pray that you would empower _____ to abstain from all sexual immorality. Protect them in their personal relationships and guard their eyes against anything that would promote or demonstrate immoral relationships. Protect them from the devastating lure of lust. Give them discernment and desire for purity, and create seriousness in their hearts concerning how they control their bodies. Father, our holiness is serious to you because you are holy. Help us to embrace the truth that to disregard your calling on our lives for purity is to disregard you. For your glory and their good, in Jesus' name, amen.

Write down any thoughts or ideas you may want to *Share*:

Day Three of Purity

Father, open my eyes so that I might *see* you more clearly, *savor* you more fully, and *share* you more freely.

Circle or underline any key words or phrases you *See*:

Do not love the world or the things in the world. If anyone loves the world, the love of the Father is not in him. For all that is in the world—the desires of the flesh and the desires of the eyes and pride of life—is not from the Father but is from the world. And the world is passing away along with its desires, but whoever does the will of God abides forever. (1 John 2:15-17)

Savor these truths in prayer for you and your student:

Father, you are clear in what is good for us and what is not. Too often our appetites lead us astray. Father, I pray that you would give _____ an appetite that causes supreme delight and enjoyment in you. Keep earthly loves from creeping into their hearts. Grant them an acute awareness of when they are being lured into the desires of the flesh. Give them eyes to see the futility in loving the things of this world. Cause their love for you to increase and abound in depth, breadth, length, and height. For your glory and their good. In Jesus' name, amen.

Write down any thoughts or ideas you may want to *Share*:

Day Four of Purity

Father, open my eyes so that I might *see* you more clearly, *savor* you more fully, and *share* you more freely.

Circle or underline any key words or phrases you *See*:

Now to him who is able to keep you from stumbling and to present you blameless before the presence of his glory with great joy, to the only God, our Savior, through Jesus Christ our Lord, be glory, majesty, dominion, and authority, before all time and now and forever. Amen. (Jude 1:24-25)

Savor these truths in prayer for you and your student:

Father, I commit _____ to you today. You alone are able to keep them from stumbling and make them blameless in your presence. Don't let them get sidetracked by sin and temptation. Capture their minds and hearts with the wonder of one day entering into the presence of your glory. Cause them to move steadily toward you and your purposes. Make them long for you and your presence. May your name be blessed and praised forever. In Jesus' name, amen.

Write down any thoughts or ideas you may want to *Share*:

Day Five of Purity

Father, open my eyes so that I might *see* you more clearly, *savor* you more fully, and *share* you more freely.

Circle or underline any key words or phrases you *See*:

Create in me a clean heart, O God, and renew a right spirit within me. Cast me not away from your presence, and take not your Holy Spirit from me. Restore to me the joy of your salvation, and uphold me with a willing spirit. (Psalm 51:10-12)

Savor these truths in prayer for you and your student:

Father, only you can create a clean heart and renew a right spirit within us. Cause _____ to be discontented until they have come to you, so that you can cleanse their hearts and renew a right spirit within them. Help them to feel the weight of their disobedience toward you. Please do not let them become comfortable with unconfessed sin in their lives. Give them a longing to be in your presence. Help them to know the Holy Spirit's leading and conviction. Grant that they would desire more than anything the restoration of the joy of your salvation. May they rejoice in the sustaining power of your Spirit. For your glory and their good, in Jesus' name, amen.

Write down any thoughts or ideas you may want to *Share*:

Day Six of Purity

Father, open my eyes so that I might *see* you more clearly, *savor* you more fully, and *share* you more freely.

Circle or underline any key words or phrases you *See*:

Now may the God of peace himself sanctify you completely, and may your whole spirit and soul and body be kept blameless at the coming of our Lord Jesus Christ. He who calls you is faithful; he will surely do it. Brothers, pray for us. (1 Thessalonians 5:23-25)

Savor these truths in prayer for you and your student:

Father, I praise you as the God of Peace. I call upon you to sanctify _____ completely. Please keep their whole spirit and body blameless before you. I stand in awe of your perfect faithfulness to your children. Thank you that you finish your work in each one of them. Don't let them wander from the truth, and help them yield to your will daily. May you enable them to embrace the sanctification process, letting go of sin and the weights that hold them back. Cause them to move forward, filled with your powerful peace. For your glory and their good, in Jesus' name, amen.

Write down any thoughts or ideas you may want to *Share*:

Day Seven of Purity

Father, open my eyes so that I might *see* you more clearly, *savor* you more fully, and *share* you more freely.

Circle or underline any key words or phrases you *See*:

Every way of a man is right in his own eyes, but the LORD weighs the heart. (Proverbs 21:2)

All the ways of a man are pure in his own eyes, but the LORD weighs the spirit. (Proverbs 16:2)

The heart is deceitful above all things, and desperately sick; who can understand it? "I the LORD search the heart and test the mind..." (Jeremiah 17:9-10)

Savor these truths in prayer for you and your student:

Father, ever since we turned from you in the garden, we have thought that our way was the best way. Your way is always best. Forgive us for being deceived in thinking that our way is ever the right way. I pray today that _____ would know the truth about their hearts. Cause them to walk humbly with you, the one who knows and understands their inmost thoughts and intentions. Transform their hearts to be in tune with you and your purposes, making them tender and teachable towards you and others. Cause them to submit to your Spirit and your Word, guiding and directing them in the way they should go. For your glory and their good, in Jesus' name, amen.

Write down any thoughts or ideas you may want to *Share*:

Notes

WEEK TEN

Speech

One of the designs of this book is to help you make praying the Scriptures for the next generation as natural as breathing. Unlike breathing, though, identifying key passages and turning them into prayers takes a little practice. In the last chapter of this book you will have the opportunity to create your own prayers. So with that in mind, I encourage you to start taking note of any words or phrases that are especially encouraging or inspiring as you are praying. Also, be on the hunt for portions of Scripture that you would like to make the focus of your prayers. Remember to ask God for his favor while you create prayers that will bless your student.

Day One of Speech

Father, open my eyes so that I might *see* you more clearly, *savor* you more fully, and *share* you more freely.

Circle or underline any key words or phrases you *See*:

Let no corrupting talk come out of your mouths, but only such as is good for building up, as fits the occasion, that it may give grace to those who hear. (Ephesians 4:29)

Let there be no filthiness nor foolish talk nor crude joking, which are out of place, but instead let there be thanksgiving. (Ephesians 5:4)

Savor these truths in prayer for you and your student:

Father, I pray that _____ would speak good words with purpose and precision. Grant that they would speak in a way that builds others up and offers grace to those who hear. Protect them from corrupt and foolish talk. Guard them from speech that is filled with filthiness and crude joking. Allow them to initiate conversations that are gracious and encouraging. Create in them gratefulness for all that you have done for them. I pray that thankfulness would flow freely from their lips so that you are glorified and others are uplifted. For your glory and their good, in Jesus' name, amen.

Write down any thoughts or ideas you may want to *Share*:

Day Two of Speech

Father, open my eyes so that I might *see* you more clearly, *savor* you more fully, and *share* you more freely.

Circle or underline any key words or phrases you *See*:

...do not be anxious about anything, but in everything by prayer and supplication with thanksgiving let your requests be made known to God. And the peace of God, which surpasses all understanding, will guard your hearts and your minds in Christ Jesus. (Philippians 4:6-7)

Savor these truths in prayer for you and your student:

Father, thank you that you are our hope in all circumstances. We do not need to be afraid or anxious, but when we are, we can come to you in prayer. Thank you for the gift of prayer. I pray today that _____ would diligently come to you in prayer in all circumstances. Help them know that you hear the words they offer up in prayer. I pray that your peace, which surpasses all understanding, would flood their hearts and minds in Christ. Your peace is powerful to guard their hearts and minds from fear and anxiety. Cause them to pray without ceasing, making it their most-used form of speech. For your glory and their good, in Jesus' name, amen.

Write down any thoughts or ideas you may want to *Share*:

Day Three of Speech

Father, open my eyes so that I might *see* you more clearly, *savor* you more fully, and *share* you more freely.

Circle or underline any key words or phrases you *See*:

Continue steadfastly in prayer, being watchful in it with thanksgiving. At the same time, pray also for us, that God may open to us a door for the word, to declare the mystery of Christ, on account of which I am in prison—that I may make it clear, which is how I ought to speak. (Colossians 4:2-4)

Savor these truths in prayer for you and your student:

Father, thank you that you have given us the opportunity to make your greatness known to the world. I pray that _____ would become effective in their ability to share the beauty of Christ. Cause them to deeply know and embrace the truth in your Word. I pray that you would open doors for them to present the truth freely and frequently. Help them to fall deeper and deeper in love with you as they read your Word. Give them clarity concerning your love and purposes for this world, and the ability to share them clearly. Give them freedom in sharing your truths no matter what setting they find themselves in. May they be steadfast in prayer, thanking you for the opportunity to advance your words of truth. For your glory and their good, in Jesus' name, amen.

Write down any thoughts or ideas you may want to *Share*:

Day Four of Speech

Father, open my eyes so that I might *see* you more clearly, *savor* you more fully, and *share* you more freely.

Circle or underline any key words or phrases you *See*:

Let your speech always be gracious, seasoned with salt, so that you may know how you ought to answer each person. (Colossians 4:6)

Savor these truths in prayer for you and your student:

Father, I ask today that you would fill _____ with your wisdom, love, faith, and purity. Help them to know that it is only through your grace that they can please you with their speech. Create in them speech that is gracious and seasoned with salt. Cause them to become a magnet for good conversation. May the words they speak also cause listeners to hunger and thirst for you and your truth. Give them deep and abiding wisdom so that their conversations will glorify you. For your glory and their good, in Jesus' name, amen.

Write down any thoughts or ideas you may want to *Share*:

Day Five of Speech

Father, open my eyes so that I might *see* you more clearly, *savor* you more fully, and *share* you more freely.

Circle or underline any key words or phrases you *See*:

Have nothing to do with foolish, ignorant controversies; you know that they breed quarrels. And the Lord's servant must not be quarrelsome but kind to everyone, able to teach, patiently enduring evil, correcting his opponents with gentleness. God may perhaps grant them repentance leading to a knowledge of the truth... (2 Timothy 2:23-25)

Savor these truths in prayer for you and your student:

Father, protect _____ today from foolish speech. Give them wisdom to know when a pointless argument is emerging in conversation. Help them to have nothing to do with speech that breeds useless quarrels. Empower them to be kind and not quarrelsome. Cause them to be filled with your loving gentleness when they have to correct others. Give them patience and clarity as they speak the knowledge of your truth. May you be praised for all the gracious ways your children speak. In Jesus' name, amen.

Write down any thoughts or ideas you may want to *Share*:

Day Six of Speech

Father, open my eyes so that I might *see* you more clearly, *savor* you more fully, and *share* you more freely.

Circle or underline any key words or phrases you *See*:

Rejoice always, pray without ceasing, give thanks in all circumstances; for this is the will of God in Christ Jesus for you. (1 Thessalonians 5:16-18)

We give thanks to God always for all of you, constantly mentioning you in our prayers... (1 Thessalonians 1:2)

Savor these truths in prayer for you and your student:

Father, thank you for clearly revealing your will for us in Christ Jesus. I pray that _____ would have a lifestyle that is marked by rejoicing, prayer, and thankfulness. Cause them to find joy in your goodness each day, and help them to express that joy through praise to you. Create in them a longing to see your greatness each day, and help them express their longing in relentless prayer. Help their prayers to be saturated with thankfulness for all things in all circumstances. Give them eyes to see the good you are doing in and through others. Cause their hearts to overflow in thankfulness toward you. For your glory and their good, in Jesus' name, amen.

Write down any thoughts or ideas you may want to *Share*:

Day Seven of Speech

Father, open my eyes so that I might *see* you more clearly, *savor* you more fully, and *share* you more freely.

Circle or underline any key words or phrases you *See*:

If anyone thinks he is religious and does not bridle his tongue but deceives his heart, this person's religion is worthless. (James 1:26)

Savor these truths in prayer for you and your student:

Father, thank you for reminding us that our speech matters! Our ability to control our words reflects the authenticity of our relationship with you. A reckless tongue reveals our need for a savior. I pray today that you would empower _____ to be diligent in controlling their tongue. Help them see how their words reveal the condition of their hearts. When their words go wayward, cause them to confess and repent. I pray that they would turn to you and the power of your Spirit for the grace to transform their hearts and speech. For your glory and their good, in Jesus' name, amen.

Write down any thoughts or ideas you may want to *Share*:

Notes

WEEK ELEVEN

Conduct

Prayer is asking God to incarnate, to get dirty in your life. Yes, the eternal God scrubs floors. For sure we know he washes feet. So take Jesus at his word. Ask him. Tell him what you want. Get dirty. Write out your prayer requests; don't mindlessly drift through life on the American narcotic of busyness. If you try to seize the day, the day will eventually break you. Seize the corner of his garment and don't let go until he blesses you. He will reshape the day. — PAUL E. MIL-LER

Humble yourselves, therefore, under the mighty hand of God so that at the proper time he may exalt you, casting all your anxieties on him, because he cares for you. (1 Peter 5:6-7)

Day One of Conduct

Father, open my eyes so that I might *see* you more clearly, *savor* you more fully, and *share* you more freely.

Circle or underline any key words or phrases you *See*:

I am the vine; you are the branches. Whoever abides in me and I in him, he it is that bears much fruit, for apart from me you can do nothing. (John 15:5)

Savor these truths in prayer for you and your student:

Father, thank you for making it clear that we are dependent on you for everything. We must rely on and abide in Jesus for our spiritual life if we are to have any hope of flourishing. Apart from you we can do nothing. It is you who sustains us and empowers us each day. Cause _____ to abide in you today. Empower them by your Spirit to bear fruit that lasts. Give them a longing to abide in you and help others to come and find their greatest satisfaction in you. For your glory and their good, in Jesus' name, amen.

Write down any thoughts or ideas you may want to *Share*:

Day Two of Conduct

Father, open my eyes so that I might *see* you more clearly, *savor* you more fully, and *share* you more freely.

Circle or underline any key words or phrases you *See*:

Therefore, since we have been justified by faith, we have peace with God through our Lord Jesus Christ. Through him we have also obtained access by faith into this grace in which we stand, and we rejoice in hope of the glory of God. Not only that, but rejoice in our sufferings, knowing that suffering produces endurance, and endurance produces character, and character produces hope, and hope does not put us to shame, because God's love has been poured into our hearts through the Holy Spirit who has been given to us. (Romans 5:1-5)

Savor these truths in prayer for you and your student:

Father, I pray that _____ would know that every challenge or trial they face has a purpose that is bigger than what they can see. Remind them that the glorious grace in which they stand is not their own. Help them to see glimpses of the character and hope you are forging in their lives. Cause them to see and savor the love that has been poured out into their hearts by the Holy Spirit. May their lips be filled with praises of the goodness that results from enduring hardships. May their hope in you always propel them forward in faith. For your glory and their good, in Jesus' name, amen.

Write down any thoughts or ideas you may want to *Share*:

Day Three of Conduct

Father, open my eyes so that I might *see* you more clearly, *savor* you more fully, and *share* you more freely.

Circle or underline any key words or phrases you *See*:

His master said to him, 'Well done, good and faithful servant. You have been faithful over a little; I will set you over much. Enter into the joy of your master.' (Matthew 25:21)

For we are his workmanship, created in Christ Jesus for good works which God prepared beforehand, that we should walk in them. (Ephesians 2:10)

Savor these truths in prayer for you and your student:

Father, you have given us natural abilities and specific personalities to accomplish your purposes. I pray that _____ would long to fulfill the purposes and desires you have for them in this life. Give them a tenacity of purpose that causes them to stay the course faithfully to the end. May your supreme purpose of faithfully and fully loving you and their neighbors be their top priorities. Help them to start well in this journey of faith with you, but more importantly I pray that you would empower them to finish well. May they hear your marvelous words: "Well done, good and faithful servant" and "Enter into the joy of your master." For your glory and their good, in Jesus' name, amen.

Write down any thoughts or ideas you may want to *Share*:

Day Four of Conduct

Father, open my eyes so that I might *see* you more clearly, *savor* you more fully, and *share* you more freely.

Circle or underline any key words or phrases you *See*:

You are the light of the world. A city set on a hill cannot be hidden. Nor do people light a lamp and put it under a basket, but on a stand, and it gives light to all in the house. In the same way, let your light shine before others, so that they may see your good works and give glory to your Father who is in heaven. (Matthew 5:14-16)

Savor these truths in prayer for you and your student:

Father, you have called us to shine in such a way that the world will know you are great. I pray that _____ would grasp the calling on their life to shine for your glory. Don't let them hide their light behind shyness or fear. Create in them courage to do works of love, kindness, mercy, and justice so that the world might be captured by your greatness. Awaken them to new ways that they can serve you and mankind that would exalt your name and goodness on earth. Give them insight on how to help others join in the joy of serving and glorifying you through their good works. May you be praised forever, in Jesus' name, amen.

Write down any thoughts or ideas you may want to *Share*:

Day Five of Conduct

Father, open my eyes so that I might *see* you more clearly, *savor* you more fully, and *share* you more freely.

Circle or underline any key words or phrases you *See*:

Live in harmony with one another. Do not be haughty, but associate with the lowly. Never be wise in your own sight. Repay no one evil for evil, but give thought to do what is honorable in the sight of all. If possible, so far as it depends on you, live peaceably with all. (Romans 12:16-18)

Savor these truths in prayer for you and your student:

Father, your call on our lives is personal and practical. Thank you for the admonitions in this passage that show us how to live a flourishing life with others. I pray that _____ would find joy in pursuing a life of harmony with others. Do not let them think more highly of themselves than they should. Help them to resist having a proud spirit. Empower them to naturally engage with those who are less fortunate than they are, knowing that everything they have is by your gracious hand. Never let them desire revenge for wrongs suffered. Give them the power of your spirit to do what is honorable in the sight of all, just as Jesus did when he unjustly suffered. Create in them a passionate desire to live at peace with everyone. For your glory and their good, in Jesus' name, amen.

Write down any thoughts or ideas you may want to *Share*:

Day Six of Conduct

Father, open my eyes so that I might *see* you more clearly, *savor* you more fully, and *share* you more freely.

Circle or underline any key words or phrases you *See*:

So whether you eat or drink, or whatever you do, do all to the glory of God. (1 Corinthians 10:31)

And whatever you do, in word or deed, do everything in the name of the Lord Jesus, giving thanks to God the Father through him. (Colossians 3:17)

Savor these truths in prayer for you and your student:

Father, thank you that our lives belong to you. You created us by your power and for your glory. It is only when we live for your glory that our lives can be fulfilled. I pray that you would draw _____ to yourself today so they would know the sweetness and power of your presence. Give them strength, desire, and passion to do everything they do today for your glory. Help them to give thanks to God in all things. Cause them to enjoy each moment of their life, knowing that it is a gift from you. Make their heart overflow with thankfulness to you in all they say and do, reminding them that you are the provider of all things. May your name be exalted by whatever they do today. For your glory and their good, in Jesus' name, amen.

Write down any thoughts or ideas you may want to *Share*:

Day Seven of Conduct

Father, open my eyes so that I might *see* you more clearly, *savor* you more fully, and *share* you more freely.

Circle or underline any key words or phrases you *See*:

But exhort one another every day, as long as it is called "today," that none of you may be hardened by the deceitfulness of sin. (Hebrews 3:13)

Savor these truths in prayer for you and your student:

Father, thank you that you do not let us just go our own way. Thank you that you care and correct us through your Word. Your correction is a demonstration of your great love for us. I pray that you would raise up friends in _____ 's life who will hold them accountable. Help them to realize that loving correction is a gift that helps protect them from sin. Remind them that deception by nature is blinding, and create in them eyes to see the deceitfulness of sin. Keep them from rebelling against the people in their lives who challenge them with the truth, and protect them from hardening their hearts to that truth. For your glory and their good, in Jesus' name, amen.

Write down any thoughts or ideas you may want to *Share*:

Notes

Praying the Proverbs

P raying the Scriptures is an exhilarating exercise that God can use to expand your heart and mind for him. As you are praying for your young friend, you will find that you may need to pray about some very practical applications of The 7 Essentials. This is where I want to encourage you to pray the Proverbs. God has given us an entire book of succinct truths that bring clarity to the practical aspects of life in the Proverbs. Fresh, vibrant, real-life issues are made crisp and clear by the wisest man to step foot on earth—not including Jesus, of course. There are thirty-one chapters, so you could pray through a chapter a day if you choose. Or, you could take your time and pray through a chapter over the course of a week. For this week, I am going to take chapter three of Proverbs and demonstrate how to pray through it. Praying through the Proverbs will eventually cover each of The 7 Essentials as you work through the thirty-one chapters. May God be praised!

Day One

Father, open my eyes so that I might *see* you more clearly, *savor* you more fully, and *share* you more freely.

Circle or underline any key words or phrases you *See*:

My son, do not forget my teaching, but let your heart keep my command-ments, for length of days and years of life and peace they will add to you. Let not steadfast love and faithfulness forsake you; bind them around your neck; write them on the tablet of your heart. So you will find favor and good success in the sight of God and man. (Proverbs 3:1-4)

Savor these truths in prayer for you and your student:

Father, I pray for _____ today, that you would keep their memories fresh and clear with the truths of your Word. Cause them to embrace your commands as daily guidance, re-sulting in long and peace-filled lives. Help them to take hold of your steadfast love and faithfulness in the forefront of their minds. May they create written reminders throughout their lives of your love and faithfulness. Show them how these have provided them favor and good success with you and man. For your glory and their good, in Jesus' name, amen.

Write down any thoughts or ideas you may want to *Share*:

Day Two

Father, open my eyes so that I might *see* you more clearly, *savor* you more fully, and *share* you more freely.

Circle or underline any key words or phrases you *See*:

Trust in the LORD with all your heart, and do not lean on your own understanding. In all your ways acknowledge him, and he will make straight your paths. Be not wise in your own eyes; fear the LORD, and turn away from evil. It will be healing to your flesh and refreshment to your bones. (Proverbs 3:5-8)

Savor these truths in prayer for you and your student:

Father, thank you for your promises. Cause _____ to have complete and unwavering trust in you and your promises today. Keep them from leaning on their own understanding which is limited and faulty. Give them the ability to see and acknowledge your working in their lives each day and trust that you will make their paths clear. Guard them against being wise in their own eyes. Cause them to fear you and turn away from even the hint of evil. Don't let them get comfortable with or delight in the slightest evil thing. Create in them a longing for holiness and righteousness that exalts you and your goodness. May you bring a wave of healing and refreshment to their bodies that would point the world to your greatness. For your glory and their good, in Jesus' name, amen.

Write down any thoughts or ideas you may want to *Share*:

Day Three

Father, open my eyes so that I might *see* you more clearly, *savor* you more fully, and *share* you more freely.

Circle or underline any key words or phrases you *See*:

Honor the LORD with your wealth and with the firstfruits of all your produce; then your barns will be filled with plenty, and your vats will be bursting with wine. My son, do not despise the LORD's discipline or be weary of his reproof, for the LORD reproves him whom he loves, as a father the son in whom he delights. (Proverbs 3:9-12)

Savor these truths in prayer for you and your student:

Father, I praise you as the provider of all things. I pray for _____, that you would enlarge their hearts for you today. Give them uncontainable pleasure in honoring you with the wealth that you have provided. Help them to know that their hope lies in you, not how much money they have in the bank. Your promises are true and you have made it clear throughout your Word that you will take care of them, as they trust you. Remind them that any season of discipline they receive from you is a sign of your absolute love for them. For your glory and their good, in Jesus' name, amen.

Write down any thoughts or ideas you may want to *Share*:

Day Four

Father, open my eyes so that I might *see* you more clearly, *savor* you more fully, and *share* you more freely.

Circle or underline any key words or phrases you *See*:

Blessed is the one who finds wisdom, and the one who gets understanding, for the gain from her is better than gain from silver and her profit better than gold. She is more precious than jewels, and nothing you desire can compare with her. Long life is in her right hand; in her left hand are riches and honor. Her ways are ways of pleasantness, and all her paths are peace. She is a tree of life to those who lay hold of her; those who hold her fast are called blessed. (Proverbs 3:13-18)

Savor these truths in prayer for you and your student:

Father, I pray for _____ today, that they would know the blessing of finding wisdom and understanding. Give them strong desires for you that propel them toward seeking wisdom and understanding. Let them taste the treasures of a life that is marked by your magnificent wisdom and understanding. May long life, riches, and honor be theirs, along with great joy as they follow your path of wisdom leading to peace and pleasantness. Cause their paths to lead to the tree of life, most specifically to the cross of Christ. It was your wisdom that made life possible in Jesus. Cause their hearts to pursue your wisdom above all else. For your glory and their good, in Jesus' name, amen.

Write down any thoughts or ideas you may want to *Share*:

Day Five

Father, open my eyes so that I might *see* you more clearly, *savor* you more fully, and *share* you more freely.

Circle or underline any key words or phrases you *See*:

The LORD by wisdom founded the earth; by understanding he established the heavens; by his knowledge the deeps broke open, and the clouds drop down the dew. My son, do not lose sight of these—keep sound wisdom and discretion, and they will be life for your soul and adornment for your neck. Then you will walk on your way securely, and your foot will not stumble. If you lie down, you will not be afraid; when you lie down, your sleep will be sweet. (Proverbs 3:19-24)

Savor these truths in prayer for you and your student:

Father, it is by your wisdom that the earth was founded and the heavens established, and for that we praise your name. I pray that _____ would see your provision in all of creation and savor the greatness of your wisdom in every blade of grass and every star above. May their hearts be encouraged by your sovereignty every time a raindrop splashes on their face. Make them tenacious in not losing sight of the preciousness of sound wisdom and discretion in everyday life. May they taste of the fruit of wisdom and discretion deep within their souls. Give them security, stability, peace, and sweetness of sleep because of it. For your glory and their good, in Jesus' name, amen.

Write down any thoughts or ideas you may want to *Share*:

Day Six

Father, open my eyes so that I might *see* you more clearly, *savor* you more fully, and *share* you more freely.

Circle or underline any key words or phrases you *See*:

Do not be afraid of sudden terror or of the ruin of the wicked, when it comes, for the LORD will be your confidence and will keep your foot from being caught. Do not withhold good from those to whom it is due, when it is in your power to do it. Do not say to your neighbor, "Go, and come again, tomorrow I will give it"—when you have it with you. (Proverbs 3:25-28)

Savor these truths in prayer for you and your student:

Father, I pray for _____ today, that they would not be fearful when bad things happen in the world. Give them a resilient confidence in you as their great Savior and Lord. May their peaceful confidence in you cause others to look to you as their hope as well. Cause them to live life with a loose grip on material things and a firm hold on you. Make them generous with their lives and resources, blessing others when it is in their power to do so. Create in them a desire and devotion to helping others in the now. Create in them an urgency to do good when they can. For your glory and their good, in Jesus' name, amen.

Write down any thoughts or ideas you may want to *Share*:

Day Seven

Father, open my eyes so that I might *see* you more clearly, *savor* you more fully, and *share* you more freely.

Circle or underline any key words or phrases you *See*:

Do not plan evil against your neighbor, who dwells trustingly beside you. Do not contend with a man for no reason, when he has done you no harm. Do not envy a man of violence and do not choose any of his ways, for the devious person is an abomination to the LORD, but the upright are in his confidence. The LORD's curse is on the house of the wicked, but he blesses the dwelling of the righteous. Toward the scorners he is scornful, but to the humble he gives favor. The wise will inherit honor, but fools get disgrace. (Proverbs 3:29-35)

Savor these truths in prayer for you and your student:

Father, all your ways are good and those who walk in your wisdom will inherit honor. I pray that _____ will walk humbly in your wisdom so they may know the sweetness of your favor and honor. Keep them from ever planning harm against others and help them to stop others from doing so as well. Make them peacemakers in their relationships. Give them eyes to see when they are becoming contentious and give them grace to turn quickly away from that path. Remind them that the devious are always at odds with you and will never receive your blessing, but those who walk uprightly will know the depth of your favor and goodness. For your glory and their good, in Jesus' name, amen.

Write down any thoughts or ideas you may want to *Share*:

Notes

Leverage Prayers

A leverage prayer is a Scripture passage that displays a prayer and effect framework. This definition may never find its way into Webster's, but it provides us with clarity as we use Scripture to pray powerfully and effectively. Leverage prayers can be identified by transitional phrases like "so that," "that you may," and "so as to." These phrases create a bridge from the prayer to the benefits of praying it. Leverage prayers are gifts from God to help us understand what can happen when we pray for specific things. Use the S3 process to make the most of these leverage prayers:

1. *See*: Identify the key components of the prayer and the benefits of the "so that" section in each prayer.

2. *Savor*: Make these prayers your own. Hover over key portions that God causes to resonate with you, and savor it in prayer for a season.

3. *Share*: Be intentional about sharing the greatness of God you are seeing and savoring in prayer with those God brings into your life. (Don't forget to read the "Ten Tips for Engaging with Teens" in the Appendix to help you with this step!)

Day One

Father, open my eyes so that I might *see* you more clearly, *savor* you more fully, and *share* you more freely.

*For this reason, because I have heard of your faith in the Lord Jesus and your love toward all the saints, I do not cease to give thanks for you, remembering you in my prayers, that the God of our Lord Jesus Christ, the Father of glory, may give you the Spirit of wisdom and of revelation in the knowledge of him, having the eyes of your hearts enlightened, **that you may** know what is the hope to which he has called you, what are the riches of his glorious inheritance in the saints, and what is the immeasurable greatness of his power toward us who believe, according to the working of his great might that he worked in Christ when he raised him from the dead and seated him at his right hand in the heavenly places, far above all rule and authority and power and dominion, and above every name that is named, not only in this age but also in the one to come. And he put all things under his feet and gave him as head over all things to the church, which is his body, the fullness of him who fills all in all. (Ephesians 1:15-23)*

Prayer:

Benefits of the prayer:

Day Two

Father, open my eyes so that I might *see* you more clearly, *savor* you more fully, and *share* you more freely.

For this reason I bow my knees before the Father, from whom every family in heaven and on earth is named, that according to the riches of his glory he may grant you to be strengthened with power through his Spirit in your inner being, so that Christ may dwell in your hearts through faith—that you, being rooted and grounded in love, may have strength to comprehend with all the saints what is the breadth and length and height and depth, and to know the love of Christ that surpasses knowledge, that you may be filled with all the fullness of God. (Ephesians 3:14-19)

Prayer:

Benefits of the prayer:

Day Three

Father, open my eyes so that I might *see* you more clearly, *savor* you more fully, and *share* you more freely.

And it is my prayer that your love may abound more and more, with knowledge and all discernment, **so that you may** *approve what is excellent, and so be pure and blameless for the day of Christ, filled with the fruit of righteousness that comes through Jesus Christ, to the glory and praise of God. (Philippians 1:9-11)*

Prayer:

Benefits of the prayer:

Day Four

Father, open my eyes so that I might *see* you more clearly, *savor* you more fully, and *share* you more freely.

*And so, from the day we heard, we have not ceased to pray for you, asking that you may be filled with the knowledge of his will in all spiritual wisdom and understanding, **so as to** walk in a manner worthy of the Lord, fully pleasing to him, bearing fruit in every good work and increasing in the knowledge of God. May you be strengthened with all power, according to his glorious might, for all endurance and patience with joy, giving thanks to the Father, who has qualified you to share in the inheritance of the saints in light. (Colossians 1:9-12)*

Prayer:

Benefits of the prayer:

Day Five

Father, open my eyes so that I might *see* you more clearly, *savor* you more fully, and *share* you more freely.

*…and may the Lord make you increase and abound in love for one another and for all, as we do for you, **so that he may** establish your hearts blameless in holiness before our God and Father, at the coming of our Lord Jesus with all his saints. (1 Thessalonians 3:12-13)*

Prayer:

Benefits of the prayer:

Day Six

Father, open my eyes so that I might *see* you more clearly, *savor* you more fully, and *share* you more freely.

To this end we always pray for you, that our God may make you worthy of his calling and may fulfill every resolve for good and every work of faith by his power, **so that the name of our Lord Jesus may** *be glorified in you, and you in him, according to the grace of our God and the Lord Jesus Christ. (2 Thessalonians 1:11-12)*

Prayer:

Benefits of the prayer:

Day Seven

Father, open my eyes so that I might *see* you more clearly, *savor* you more fully, and *share* you more freely.

*Now may the God of peace who brought again from the dead our Lord Jesus, the great shepherd of the sheep, by the blood of the eternal covenant, equip you with everything good **that you may** do his will, working in us that which is pleasing to his sight, through Jesus Christ, to whom be glory forever and ever. Amen. (Hebrews 13:20-21)*

Prayer:

Benefits of the prayer:

Notes

APPENDIX

Ten Tips for Engaging with Teens

B ridging the gap between generations can be challenging and intimidating—no matter what age you are—so here are a few tips to help you begin that process with ease:

1. *Be in prayer for God's favor in the relationship.* One of my favorite prayers in Scripture is when Nehemiah finds out the walls are broken down around Jerusalem and the city is vulnerable. He wants to help and prays for favor with the King of Persia in chapter one, which he concludes with the following words: "O Lord, let your ear be attentive to the prayer of your servant, and to the prayer of your servants who delight to fear your name, and give success to your servant today, and grant him mercy in the sight of this man." Just as Nehemiah covered his relationships in prayer, we too should approach any new relationship this way.

2. *Be prepared.* Collect several key questions that will help you engage with your student. Questions are one of

the best tools for communication, and asking the right ones will be invaluable as you seek to learn more about your student. You must also genuinely care about the life of the teenager you are praying for. You have to believe that they have information or life stories that are worthwhile and meaningful. Be ready to take on the role of listener as you get to know your student better.

3. *Understand the power of good questions.* Most encounters with your student will be short, so you will want to make the most of your time with them. Ask questions that open the door to good conversation. These types of questions will likely be easy to answer and will not make the student feel as if there is a "right" answer to give. For example, you could ask, "What were some of your favorite parts of the weekend retreat?" rather than asking, "What was the best part of the weekend retreat?" Giving the student freedom to reply with more answers and more information will help the conversation flow more naturally.

4. *Always ask how you can pray.* Make it a habit to ask: "What is the best way I can be praying for you this week?" If they are stumped, ask them what things are coming up in their week. Be sure to let them know what passage of Scripture you are praying for them that week too.

5. *Building the relationship takes time.* So, when you see your friend at church, engage—ask a couple questions about their week, and then let the friendship grow at its own pace throughout the year.

You can offer the student the option to contact you

with anything they would like special prayer about. This way, you are opening up the lines of communication to them. If you are on Facebook, or any other social media site, I would encourage you not to "friend" your student. Let them make that move if they want to. Your goal is to connect in a way that seems natural and does not make them feel awkward in any way.

6. *Be alert when you pray.* Take note of things that God may bring to your mind as you pray the Scriptures for your student and perhaps write a short note to them encouraging them with that passage.

7. *Affirm your student!* Look for natural ways to encourage them during conversations. Pay attention to how God is working in their lives and affirm the good things you see. Over time, let them know the areas in which you've seen them grow.

8. *Collect stories.* Begin thinking about how God has worked in your life through his Word and his people. Collect several stories of where you have seen God show up in your life. Think of how you saw God's faithfulness at work during different stages of your life too. As your friendship grows, God can open up avenues for you to be able to share your story. This is a very clear way to fulfill Psalm 71:17-18:

O God, from my youth you have taught me, and I still proclaim your wondrous deeds. So even to old age and gray hairs, O God, do not forsake me, until I proclaim your might to another generation, your power to all those to come.

9. *Pray with other Prayer Champions.* Consider gathering together with your student's other Prayer Champions as you pray through the guide. This will encourage you all in your partnership for this young person. God will bless the gathering of his people in prayer. May the Lord be pleased to bless all the prayers prayed for the next generation.

10. *Join the Prayer Champion community!* Make sure to register on **www.prayformecampaign.com** to receive regular tips on connecting with your teen effectively and naturally.

What's Next?

Take the next step and become a Movement Champion today. A Movement Champion is a supporter of the Pray for Me Campaign who does three simple things:

1. **Pray.** Movement Champions pray for the advancement of the Campaign.
2. **Share.** Movement Champions spread the word about the Campaign.
3. **Give.** Movement Champions give at least $10/month to the Campaign.

Your role helps bring the greatness of God to the next generation and makes the difference in student's lives. Become a Movement Champion today!

www.prayformecampaign.com/give

50230055R00089

Made in the USA
Columbia, SC
04 February 2019